To Friends Mickey & Karen Smith
LIVE Simple, LIVE WELL, LIVE LONG.

What readers are saying about
The Biggest Lie Ever Believed.

"Mike, by education, isn't a politician, or an economist, or a historian; thank goodness. He is however, honest, intelligent and funny! He wraps common sense logic around a very real problem and presents it with witty humor. He then provides solutions. What else could you ask for?"
Judi Kohn, former teacher and currently a senior environmental & permitting technician.

"At first I was totally entertained in the down home, humorous way a dry subject was presented until I realized he wasn't kidding! Then, I hoped he was wrong, but for the life of me, I couldn't see where!"
David Mitchell, real estate broker, entrepreneur.

"If you are finding happiness in debt — don't read this book!"
ZU VIEL GUT IST SCHLECHT — German for:
Too Much Good Is Bad.
"An exhilarating, humorous book filled with irrefutable logic about where you may be heading financially. Mike's book effectively conveys the fact that living beyond your means and not teaching your children wise money habits dooms one to failure, but even worse, your children also. Finally, a goal without a plan is merely a wish."
Robert J. Heid (Ret.) Financial & Estate Planner

THE BIGGEST LIE EVER BELIEVED

By Michael Folkerth

LIFETIME CHRONICLE PRESS

Montrose, CO

First edition
Printed in the United States of America

Library of Congress Control Number: 2007929060

ISBN-13: 978-0-9779965-3-7
ISBN-10: 0-9779965-3-0

Cover illustration by David Rowe, Design Source
Book design by Laurie Goralka Design

Published by:
Lifetime Chronicle Press
121 N. Park Ave.
Montrose, CO 81401
970-240-1345
chronicle@montrose.net

DEDICATION

I dedicate this book to my wife and best friend Cathy, who remains perpetually supportive (and seemingly unscathed) by my endless ranting and raving directed at the injustices in our system. And, also for her unwavering love for a man who is eternally inflicted with an unexplainable attraction to the dismal science of economics.

TABLE OF CONTENTS

PREFACE

LIFE IS GOOD IN THE U.S.A. The stock market is at record levels, inflation is reported to be low, and on a clear day, I can see retirement on the not-so-distant horizon. The house and cars are paid for, the kids are raised and doing fine, and the grandkids are happy and healthy. Maybe just the Mrs. and I will take a cruise this year to experience a little pre-retirement bliss. We can sample a taste of our soon-to-be fulltime lifestyle of reaping the rewards for all of those years of work and planning.

All of this, and yet there was that incessant gnawing in the pit of my stomach. Something continually whispered that all wasn't quite as well as being reported by our illustrious elected officials and the scorekeepers on Wall Street. But surely they weren't lying...

I had to find out what it was that wouldn't let me peacefully bask in the nearing golden promise of retirement. And, find out I did. Can you recall the emotions that you experience when you first learn of a terrible tragedy? A tragedy such as 9-11-01, hurricane Katrina, or the loss of a loved one? If you are like me, your first instinct is to call friends and family to both alarm them of the situation and to console one another in the terrible and unthinkable reality of the moment.

It was with this level of passion and urgency that I have written this book. But, this time, the intent is to avoid another disaster rather than to report one. I wish to help you avoid an economic disaster that the majority of middle-class America is well on its way to.

When I first began this writing, I was, to say the least, angry with the politicians for the years of telling and re-telling "The Biggest Lie Ever Believed." Americans deserve better from our esteemed business leaders, those politicians in Washington, those at your state capitol, and for that matter, at your local city hall.

After completing and then re-reading the first four chapters, I realized that the anger and contempt that I felt (and still do) for our elected officials and big business leaders was being transferred to each page. So, figuring you didn't want to read the words of some fuming madman, I started over with a new conviction and a better attitude. I have tried my best to sweeten the proverbial bitter pill with humor, while at the same time providing you with verifiable information that could change your life in a very positive way.

You will note the purposeful absence of footnotes and references to scientific and economic studies. Logic, reason, common sense, fairness, and mathematics need little such borrowed acceptance.

As research was conducted and the dots were connected for writing a book of this nature, I was educated in unexpected areas. It is my sincere hope that you can take from this book all that I have personally learned while writing it.

"We the people" will prevail. After all, this is still America and we are in charge, it says so in the rules.

Mike Folkerth

INTRODUCTION

THE AMERICAN DREAM, and the American Reality, are very different. The first truly is a dream; the second is a probable nightmare. A continual promise by our nation's political, financial, and business leaders for endless economic growth, accompanied by ever greater consumption and wealth, is the third biggest lie ever told (right behind "the check's in the mail," and "we'll take a nice vacation next year"). The promise of endless economic growth, however, ranks as an absolute standout for the #1 *most believed* lie ever told — proof being that millions of American families have put their trust and faith in that assurance; a promise that plainly cannot be kept.

So why would our leaders knowingly steer us down a dead-end road? Our leaders aren't planning to ride on our bus. They're taking the limo. And, it isn't a dead-end road at all for the upper echelons of our society. High-ranking American politicians and Big Business leaders bask in a life of implausible wealth and privilege. They plan on continuing that lifestyle long after the American Dream hits the proverbial wall. But, in the meantime, the lap of luxury is provided by the great majorities' continual belief that the American Dream is alive and well — without end.

It is US then, who facilitate the lifestyle of the rich and famous simply because WE want to believe the biggest lie ever told so badly that we simply don't question the feasibility of our current lifestyle to continue. "Oh, so now it's our fault huh?" I would never have brought this up had you not asked, but indirectly, yes, it most definitely is our fault, including yours truly.

In a nutshell, "The Biggest Lie Ever Believed" is that endless growth is possible. It isn't. And yet, endless growth and, more importantly, *exponential* (ever expanding) endless growth is the very cornerstone of *your* future. Do *you* believe the "Biggest Lie Ever Believed?" Let's go find out. And if you do determine that you have been duped, it's never too late to exercise your right to freedom of speech, as in, "take this plan and shove it." This is still America, and in America anything is possible with the right plan.

All sage knowledge and advice does not come from institutions of higher learning, nor from corporate heads residing high above the big city sprawls, or for that matter, politicians (I get the idea that this doesn't surprise you). Most of the truly memorable advice that I have received thus far in life has come from those common people whose real life experiences and homespun wisdom presented me with both sound reason and unexpected perspective. Such wisdom as, "Never get mad at a person because they are smarter than you; it isn't their fault."

My goal in this book is to demonstrate three things:

One, that the economy cannot maintain status quo if predicated on exponential growth, which it is.

Two, that buying things that we don't need, with money that we don't have, is absolutely contrary to happiness, regardless of what the incessant claims of advertisers are.

And three, that there is still a way to live simply and live well in America, regardless of the inevitable decline that will take place in our current economic system.

CHAPTER 1

ECONOMICS 101, THE GREAT ILLUSION

"ELECT ME FOR GROWTH!" shouted the politician with the fervor of a faith healer. "I will bring you prosperity, more jobs, higher pay, better education, and a brighter future for my children's children." "Didn't you mean a brighter future for *our* children?" questioned a man in the front. "Them, too," came the practiced reply. Sound familiar? Sure it does. This is the same rhetoric that every candidate from President of the United States to small town Mayor has shouted since our political time began.

"A chicken in every pot and a car in every garage" was a 1928 presidential campaign slogan for Herbert Hoover, and the voters considered this a reasonable offer, giving Mr. Hoover the nod to occupy the White House. I'm confident that President Hoover would have produced those cars and chickens had he not run into a little snag in 1929 that is commonly referred to as the "Great Depression." It is of historical mention that this is also the period in time that the chicken and car motto gave way to the more graphical, "Didn't have a pot to pee in or a window to throw it out of."

Herbert Hoover's administration may have failed to come through with the goods, but his supporters did have the right idea for getting votes — promise a chicken even if you can only deliver feathers. Not a whole lot has changed since, with the exception of the booty pledged. Think about that. Would you fall for a slogan promising one car and a chicken? Not even. Now give us three cars, a garage to match, and a gift certificate to Applebee's, and we're talking.

"So what's so wrong with pledging to provide all of these amenities?" I hear you ask. "More is what we want. Haven't you ever heard of the American Dream?" Yes, I have. And therein lies the basis of the problem — the endless quest for the illusive American Dream, and the endless promises to help you capture that greatest of illusions. No one was ever elected by promising less, or for that matter, the same. More is the key and more you will be promised, regardless of the known inability to keep those assurances.

I haven't always had an interest in history and economics. My past educators would gladly attest to that fact. My third grade teacher was particularly mean-spirited and told my parents at a P.T.A. meeting that not only did I not know much, she seriously doubted that I even suspected anything. Okay, I was a slow starter. It was later in life that my interest in economics was peaked by certain historical events that I was, shall we say, fully involved in. The recession of the 1980s garnered my complete and undivided attention. How could everything have seemed to be going so well, and then WHAM, America took a $2 trillion trip downhill?

To more graphically characterize the latter statement, imagine your trip thus far through life as floating lazily down a peaceful river, when a more observant person on the boat asks, "What is that roaring sound?" That roaring sound, as it turns out, is going to be your opportunity to get an up close and personal view of the 10th Natural Wonder of the World — Niagara Falls. In this case, I want to be the person on your boat that says, "What is that noise?", while well upstream from the falls, just in case you want to dock prior to the sudden drop.

After the aforementioned economic event, I vowed never to let something the size of an elephant sneak up on me again. There had to have been signs of the downturn well before we reached the falls, and there were. I, along with most of the people in America, just didn't see it coming. This time around, I can see it in full living color.

It was in the late summer of 1992 while having coffee at the ranch of friend, Gary Swanson, that the question occurred to me. "Gary, why do Bill Clinton and George Bush both agree with the need for NAFTA?" NAFTA was the acronym for the heavily contested North American Free Trade Agreement, better known as, what borders? Gary pondered the question for a moment and admitted that he wasn't sure, but now that I had brought it up, it did seem curiously strange.

Bill Clinton and George Bush (George senior) didn't agree on whether it gets dark at night, let alone the subject of international trade policy. While Gary Swanson was best known for being one of the premier wildlife artists in the world, I knew him to be the most politically astute of my friends. Gary, as they say, had connections and could always be counted on to come up with acceptable answers to my most puzzling political questions. But not *that* question, not even with the assistance of specially formulated brain food (primarily in the form of a dozen or so of Gary's wife Andy's homemade cookies) could we pummel the subject to submission. It was a mystery, and everyone loves a mystery.

Figuring that Mr. Bush and Mr. Clinton had to be up to something of interest, I continued to ask the same question of many of my other friends and business acquaintances, all of whom responded that they didn't know, and frankly didn't care, as long as it didn't affect football season. Early one quiet morning it came to me what it was that George and Bill were equally concerned about. America's economic engine was making one of those knocking sounds that your mechanic loves to hear. But more importantly, this was an economic engine that neither Mr. Clinton nor Mr. Bush wanted to be responsible for when it blew up.

NAFTA, as it turned out, was the best idea that either one of them had for getting a few more miles from a tired economic engine, and the fact that neither one knew who was going to win the election, made for strange bedfellows. Retired politicians like to say things like, "I don't know what happened, it was alright when I left." They say this, counting on the American public not remembering what was going on the day before yesterday. They haven't got a thing to worry about — yet.

I'm getting ahead of myself here. I need to better explain my economic ride over Niagara Falls that I mentioned earlier. Years before I had ever concerned myself with what George Herbert Walker Bush and William Jefferson Clinton were up to, I had determined that our national economic model was something less than perfect. In 1977, Jimmy Carter, being a very successful Georgia peanut farmer, had taken Herbert Hoover's slogan and replaced the chickens to an unlimited supply of peanuts for every American, if we would simply elect him President. That seemed like a reasonable trade at the time. As it turned out, what Mr. Carter had really meant was that soon every American would be *working* for peanuts.

Mr. Carter was running against the incumbent Gerald Ford, who had more or less fallen into the job when his boss Richard Nixon, the President, had effectively gotten fired. Gerald Ford had been appointed to the Vice President's job when the original Vice President, Spiro T. Agnew, saw the wisdom in quitting prior to the being fired process. I have never understood why Mr. Agnew quit. There were only about 30 people in the country who actually knew that he was the Vice President. I once overheard two ladies talking and one said, "Did you know that Spiro T. Agnew is coming to town?" The other said, "Oh, great! I just got over the Asian influenza."

At any rate, once Richard Nixon got the boot, it was pointed out to Gerald that he had been serving as Vice President, and was now the President of the United States. Running against Gerald Ford proved a distinct advantage for Jimmy Carter. This advantage was never more evident than during the three debates in which he engaged Mr. Ford and handily won. In November 1976, having no idea at this point that the peanuts weren't going to come through, America elected Jimmy Carter as our 39th President.

Most campaign rhetoric and promises are forgotten at approximately 15 minutes past inauguration. Unfortunately for him, Mr. Carter had made quite a big to-do over an index (much of which was his own making) that he called the "Misery Index." It was a simple little method of determining just how much misery the good citizens were enduring at any given time by adding together the rates of unemployment and inflation; the higher the number, the higher the misery. During Jimmy's initial run for the White House, the Misery Index was 13.57%, to which he said, "No man responsible for giving the country a Misery Index this high has a right to even ask to be President." He was right. When Mr. Carter was campaigning for re-election in 1980 the Misery Index was 21.98%, and he left office saying, "What did I tell you?"

During the four years that Jimmy Carter was President, the Arabs had cut off our oil, the Iranians were holding our U.S. Embassy staff hostage, the Russians were invading Afghanistan (even though Jimmy had told them not to), nominal interest rates approached 20%, and inflation was setting new altitude records. As if that weren't enough, in 1980, Fidel Castro sent 125,000 unannounced Cuban refugees to Florida as a going out-of-office present for Mr. Carter.

By the end of his fourth year in the White House, Jimmy Carter wasn't having any fun at all. The general public was getting somewhat agitated and beginning to suspect that he wasn't the right man for the job. Sensing for the first time that he may need a little assistance, in August of 1979, the President hired Paul Volcker to act as Chairman of the Federal Reserve. Mr. Carter asked Paul Volcker to do something about the high inflation. Mr. Volcker took him seriously.

Okay, now this is a big one. If printing oodles of money creates inflation, take a wild guess at what *not* printing money does. It ain't rocket science. Mr. Volcker, shall we say, tightened the money supply, as in, shut down the press. Inflation fell like a dropped rock and interest rates followed, as did gainful employment (you can't keep your cake and eat it too). The banks, mortgage companies, and Federal Government became the largest homeowners in America, and the economic scene in general was a little rough around the edges.

I have no doubt that Jimmy Carter hadn't actually planned for the events that took place on his watch, and therefore didn't have much of a plan as to what to do when the events that he hadn't planned for actually materialized. This little oversight is often referred to in methodological terms as "poor planning, at best." This period in time is very memorable to me (my doctor calls it "post-traumatic flashback"), and marks the point where I first suspected that we were enjoying an unsustainable economic model.

This was also the same time that I was taking my financial plunge over Niagara Falls, which as I stated, had peaked my interest in economics. That being said, in 1984 my worst suspicions proved correct when the economy that I was enjoying wasn't sustainable any longer, and I went broke.

They say the difference between a recession and a depression is that during a recession, your neighbor is out of work, and during a depression, you are. In my case, about 10,000 of my Alaskan neighbors joined me for the fun, and we all witnessed a dandy little depression of enduring quality. I want to pass on a tidbit of potentially useful advice. If you find yourself considering selling a home in an area where 1,200 similar houses are vacant, take the money that you were going to use for advertising and buy food.

By this juncture I was receiving my Masters from the Baptism by Fire Institute for higher education. I had now become fully confident that the need for a major adjustment to our economic model had moved up on the "things to do today" list, from important, to mandatory. It was even more evident that Jimmy knew of what he spoke regarding the Misery Index — I was miserable. And if there is any truth to the saying "misery loves company," love was abundant across this great land.

Making the necessary adjustment to turn this mess around was not a job for the faint of heart. You see, we live in sort of an awkward situation to talk about. So awkward in fact that it is a national secret. Well, there I go; I've let the cat out of the bag. Okay, I'll tell you, but try not to spread this around. This national secret that I hinted about is that we need for more people to buy things this year than the people who bought things last year, or pretty soon everyone will have all the things they need and won't buy anything else. I'm not talking about toilet paper and toothpaste, but important things like Ford and Chevy automobiles and Beanie Babies.

The situation becomes particularly annoying when you are employed by the company that makes the things that aren't needed any longer. This set of circumstances results in a complex economic conundrum, referred to as, "an imbalance in the quantity of goods being produced on the supply side, as compared to that of current orders being generated on the demand side." Or in the case of the people who make the things that everyone already has, a condition referred to by government statisticians as, "extended unemployment." If enough people become involved in extended unemployment, it's called a "depression." The chances of being re-elected during a depression are what we in the west refer to as slim and none, and Slim left town. You can see where this is going, can't you? That's right, "Elect me for growth." Amen.

Now friends, when this little national secret gets out of register, and extended unemployment appears to have some record-setting potential, America's politicians begin to have health issues. They have visions (you may call them nightmares) of personally becoming involved in extended unemployment, and it makes them sick to think about it. To counteract this horrible possibility, a few minor adjustments need to be made to policy. Not doing so could go against the politician's last campaign promise: "My grandfather was a politician, my father was a politician, I'm a politician, and my boy ain't going to work either!" I call these adjustments to policy, *culinary accounting practices*, or as you may refer to it, *cooking the books*.

To spur consumption, we need consumers, and we need consumers NOW. So if all the current consumers are doing their part, where do we get additional shoppers? Now here's a flash. Have you ever wondered why *legal* immigration has increased year after year, even after you submitted that nasty note against the practice to the letters-to-the-editor column? Why the borders aren't guarded all that well, even though everyone at the hairdresser's agrees that they should be? Why Congress doesn't listen to all of us screaming, "WHAT IS UP WITH THIS IMMIGRATION THING? ENOUGH ALREADY!"

So, if the voting public is vocally upset over the number of *legal* immigrants, and yet more consumers are needed immediately, if not sooner, to keep the economy on track, take a guess at why nothing is done about *illegal* immigration. Whoa! I was nearly blinded by the lights coming on out there! "Surely," you say, "it's not to increase the number of people needed to consume more stuff than we consumed last year?" Go figure. Think NAFTA here. Not just yet, we are in 1979 at this point, and there are still a few rabbits left in the political magician's hat. I heard what you said, "You could have gone all day without telling us that."

For the moment, what America needed was a new leader that would make a few major adjustments to policy before the whole shebang slipped over the falls. By 1980, unelectable-itis was spreading at near epidemic levels among the Democratic politicians. Definitely a wide opening had availed itself to the Republicans, who had found just the man to do the job: Ronald Reagan.

By the time that the presidential campaign tour rolled around, Jimmy Carter's total approval rating consisted of his wife, Rosalynn, daughter Amy, and brother Billy. You may recall the Misery Index? So did Ronald Reagan. Ron felt compelled to remind all the good citizens (who were more than miserable) what Mr. Carter had said. Backed by millions of dollars in campaign contributions, as compared to the $500 that Mr. Carter's mother, Miss Lillian, had loaned Jimmy against peanut futures, Ronald Reagan mounted a brilliant campaign strategy; Ron promised that he wouldn't do whatever it was that Jimmy had been doing. Ronald Reagan was ushered in with great fanfare. This is probably the only election that Ross Perot or Ralph Nader ever had a shot at winning.

I suggested earlier that we needed leadership to encourage a whole lot more folks to become involved in the ownership of frivolous nonessentials, or oatmeal could become standard fare for dinner. Ronald Reagan was that man, to be sure. He was confident of a quick resolution, bolstered by his past acting career in Hollywood, where he had experienced hundreds of last-minute successes in saving the day by snatching the heroine out of harm's way and pounding the bejesus out of the bad guys. After all, America's economy *and* Hollywood were both based on fiction.

Mr. Reagan quickly appointed a committee to study both the cause and effect of unemployment. Within six months, the committee had spent a little more than ten-million dollars, and came to the important conclusion that most people were unemployed because they didn't have a job. The committee also reported another important discovery — unemployed people are poor and don't buy plastic flowers or pet rocks. "Ha! Just as I suspected all along," Mr. Reagan concluded. "If these people had jobs, they wouldn't be unemployed."

Now that the root of the problem was evident, it was simply a matter of putting all those unemployed voters back to work. That's no step for a stepper. Ronald hadn't always been a Republican, and was a student of Franklin Roosevelt's strategy for pulling the country out of the Great Depression. Franklin Roosevelt had won his first election much the same way as Ronald had defeated Jimmy Carter. He had beaten Herbert Hoover handily in 1932, due to Herbert's not coming through with the cars and chickens.

Ronald Reagan had been particularly impressed with Roosevelt's ability to spend enormous amounts of government money during a period in time when the government didn't *have* any money. Mr. Roosevelt was a wealthy, New-York born, Harvard/Columbia-educated lawyer, who had chosen lifelong government service as a profession to avoid gainful employment. For a man of these qualifications, "fixing the system" had seemed a minor challenge. Mr. Roosevelt's now-historical "New Deal" for creating commerce was so successful that it is still practiced in nearly every American household today. It's called "unsecured credit."

Mr. Roosevelt had seen the opportunity to make a few policy changes that were pure genius. He effectively took America off the gold standard by making it illegal for citizens to own gold. After all the gold was collected from the good people, Mr. Roosevelt directed that the value of gold be changed from $20.67 to $35.00 an ounce. You can see where this could be a good thing for the holder of all the gold, which was the Federal Government. Remember the golden rule, "He who has the gold, rules."

Mr. Roosevelt also issued an order forbidding banks to make payments in gold, and instead, payment was to be made with paper money, called "fiat currency." Fiat is technically described as "money that is current or legal tender as satisfaction for money debts by government fiat, that is, by law."

Let me clarify that last sentence about fiat money. What Mr. Roosevelt did was to create money that had no redemption value in some other form, such as gold. This unique new system allowed money to be printed without the burdensome obligation of producing collateral other than an I.O.U. Franklin then took the liberty of signing the I.O.U. "John Q. Public." No! It isn't forgery if accompanied by sufficient genius, and resulting in bringing an entire nation out of poverty. As Will Rogers said, "It is awful hard to get people interested in corruption unless they can get some of it." In this instance, 13 million unemployed people were about to get some of it. Enough said.

To fully understand this important policy change, imagine being able to draw money out of your checking account without actually putting any in, while at the same time, making your brother-in-law responsible for the overdraft. I said "imagine," because you can't actually do that. The main difference between you as an individual getting a loan and the Federal Government getting a loan is that one of you is required to pay it back. Now that Mr. Roosevelt had removed the pesky requirement of having collateral prior to printing money, he hired everyone in America to work for the Federal Government and put the bill on the cuff (called the "National Debt"). Mr. Roosevelt had set the stage not only for America's new economic model, but unbeknownst to him, had also created the model for Visa and MasterCard.

Getting back to Mr. Reagan who figured if it worked for Franklin Roosevelt, it would work for him. Mr. Reagan ran the National Debt up from about $800 billion to a little north of $2 trillion during his eight years in office, which as I said earlier, is no step for a stepper. Ron was stoking the nation's economic fire with good old American greenbacks. Military spending was pushed through the roof and dramatic income-tax reductions were legislated. Generous investment tax credits became available for business and industry concerns willing to make investments in the machinery and technology that were used in places where unemployed people got jobs; this guy was no dummy. Ronald Reagan had the "buy now and pay later" plan down to a science.

The Middle East and Russia, who had made life so difficult for Jimmy Carter, had seen enough Ronald Reagan cowboy movies to know that if you mess with the bull, you get the horns. Ronald Reagan had proven that he was not a man who gave quarters to bad guys. The Middle East and Russian leaders didn't want to risk being hog-tied and thrown in the calaboose, a fate bestowed on the villains that had crossed Ronald in the movies. Not to mention that the oil embargo had embarrassingly shorted the amount of oil being purchased from the Middle East to a point that the sheiks and war-lords were having some difficulty enjoying the lifestyle to which they had become so fondly accustomed. The oil and the money once again began flowing like an artesian well with no end in sight, and America was off like a jet.

In 1989, after eight years of service, Ronald Reagan left office with the highest approval rating of any departing President. I'll translate that for you: "More is what we wanted, and Mr. Reagan came through with the mother lode." And so Ronald Reagan rode off into the sunset and we all lived happily ever after. Well, not exactly. I'll get to that part in the next chapter. What it did do for Ronald Reagan, however, was the same thing that it did for Franklin Roosevelt's legacy. Ron could now say, "I don't know what the heck they did, it was alright when I left."

CHAPTER 2

ECONOMICS 201, IF IT'S NOT BROKE, BY ALL MEANS, BREAK IT!

I COULD TAKE YOU FURTHER BACK on our little history tour, but I think everyone is starting to get the big picture, and it appears to be a disaster movie. If America doesn't keep growing, the Great American Dream will without a doubt become the Great American Nightmare. And, since infinite growth is mathematically impossible in a finite world, it's not a matter of *if* the wheels come off, it's a matter of *when.*

I want to reiterate that I keep this thing simple for two reasons: One is that if I wrote it, it has to be simple; and two is that the subject is not all that complicated once broken down to a more comprehensive level.

Our American financial system is called Capitalism. Broken down, that is *Capital-ism,* "Capital," of course, meaning Washington, D.C., and "ism," meaning (work with me here) "isthem" people who have the capital. Two other terms that we need to become familiar with before we go on are the Federal Mint and the Bureau of Engraving and Printing. Broken down, that is *Fed-eral,* "Fed" is the abbreviation for the actual people who determine whether or not you get any capital, and "eral" (pronounced Earl) is the actual guy who is in charge of the Mint and the printing press building. MINT, which is an acronym for **M**oney **I**n **N**o **T**ime, is where the machines are kept that stamp out coins, and the Bureau of Engraving and Printing is where the paper "fiat" money is printed.

I know that I promised not to take you back any further on the history tour, but this fiat money issue is important to understand and has its roots back a little before Franklin Roosevelt's time.

We talked about the Federal Reserve Board or the "Fed," which was actually created in 1913 to act as the nation's central bank. The Fed determines the level of need for fiat currency and, in turn, directs Earl to print money, called Federal Reserve Notes (we call them "cash"). The Fed also determines how much interest they are going to charge the local member banks for loaning the banks money. The local bank then loans you the same money that the Fed loaned them, but charges you more interest than they are paying the Fed. This works out extraordinarily well for the bank, if you are kind enough to pay them back.

It is easy to see how the Fed works when loaning money to the banks and charging interest. However, the Fed also needs to print a little extra money for incidentals, such as paying salaries for government employees, remodels at the White House, and sending foreign aid to countries who, only the year before, were trying to blow us up.

Government charging interest to themselves to cover these incidentals was a problem before 1913, due mainly to the fact that the government didn't have a means to pay the principal back, let alone the interest. The complexities of explaining our monetary system would consume volumes. I will attempt to condense those volumes into two sentences. If you'll remember, the Fed was created in 1913. The 16th Amendment was also ratified in 1913, more commonly known as the Individual Graduated Federal Income Tax. That should clear up any questions that you may have had regarding where the Government would get the money not only to pay interest, but to fund government as we know it today. And so, the Fed, the Bureau of Printing and Engraving, the Mint, and the forerunners of the IRS became one big happy family. Progress can be painful.

Prior to having the modern-day Federal Mint and the Bureau of Engraving and Printing, the citizens kept running out of money as a result of spending it. You may remember that we dealt with this problem in Chapter 1. Let's recap the situation that occurs the day after people run out of money. Who can answer that? That is certainly accurate, but what happens other than the President having to move out of the White House? Exactly —— it's called a "depression." Does anyone remember what the little policy adjustment was that Franklin Roosevelt made to avoid the annoyance of him personally having to move unexpectedly? Correct, he hired Earl, and those printing presses haven't seen a day off since. More money, more consumption — how simple can it be?

Our entire economy is based on ever greater consumption. And are we good or what? Americans have taken gold, silver, bronze, and pot metal at the Consumer Olympics since the inception of the games. Just when some copycat country thinks they may be gaining on us, it's election time, the plunder promised during the campaign goes up, and we pass those foreign countries like a freight train passing a bum. All of this magnificent glory wouldn't be possible without the two-party system; regardless of what the party in charge offers, the other party who *wants* to be in charge (like, really, really wants to be charge) simply offers more.

Upping the ante, however, does not necessarily guarantee that the incumbent party will be ousted. Oh, no. The party who is currently in charge, really, really wants to REMAIN in charge and isn't about to roll over for a few billion dollars here or there. Consequently, each party continues to trump the other's offer right up to Election Day. What a wonderful system. On Election Day, the voters, who really, really want more, have to make a choice. And, as they say in the real estate business, may the best offer win.

There have been occasions where a President is coming through with so much loot that we elect him to a second term in order not to take the chance that their opponent may be fibbing — a bird in hand, so to speak.

Regardless, in America we only allow a President to hang around for a maximum of eight years, even if they have been paying off like a busted slot machine. It is of note that U.S. Presidents weren't always term limited to eight years. You history buffs may remember a guy named George Washington who was an exceptionally popular President. After his first two terms,

G.W. was asked to run again. Mr. Washington respectfully declined the gracious offer, stating that, "Two terms of four years each are enough for any President."

George Washington, due largely to living in a different century, had not had the pleasure of meeting any Harvard lawyers, let alone one, Franklin D. Roosevelt. Franklin had never had enough of nothing. After serving eight years, Mr. Roosevelt decided that he definitely hadn't had enough of being President. The food was good and the rent was right, so he ran again, and won. After serving his third four-year term, WWII was underway and he felt he couldn't abandon the country (or the White House), and won a fourth term.

Are you starting to see a pattern here? It was accepted tradition, not law, which had limited every President's term prior to Mr. Roosevelt to a maximum of eight years. There was, however, a law that prohibited any deceased person from serving as President for more than one term. It was this very rule (the "deceased rule") that ended Mr. Roosevelt's tenure after serving 13 years in the White House. It was after Mr. Roosevelt's occupancy that the popular Homesteading Act was designed.

Fearing that the next President may try and take up permanent residence at the White House, also known as the Permanent President System (P.P.S.), a law was passed in 1947 and ratified in 1951 to prohibit a President from serving more than two terms. There are two reasons for this enactment: one, after eight years, sitting Presidents are sitting on a whole lot of money and power and they don't give a hang what *you* want; and two, this rule knocks the countries that have dictators or P.P.S. systems completely out of the running for a medal in the Consumer Olympics.

It is vital to understand why the one-party dictator, or P.P.S. systems, would be a downer for the U.S. economy. Dictators only have to be elected once, after which they can remain in office for somewhere around a hundred years, or until the deceased rule kicks in. Most dictators go with tried and true methods for being elected the first time around by running on a platform that offers voter incentives, such as "Everyone who votes for me won't be shot." These types of incentives, coupled with the fact that their opponent was recently found to be dead, fairly well guarantees election. Once in office the simplified dictator tax system, i.e., "How much did you make? Send it in," makes them filthy rich within two weeks and life is good.

This economic model is not conducive to high consumption amongst the general populace and nearly rules out any prospect for attracting Wal-Mart and Home Depot. It also rules out any possibility for dictatorships to catch on in America. While employing death threats may enjoy some initial vote-getting success in the United States, once they came to the part about closing Wal-Mart and Home Depot, they would be flirting with the distinct possibility of being the opponent who was recently found to be very dead. Let's face it: there are some things worth fighting for.

Now that we can see the indispensable value of the two-party system, we also need to pay homage to those common people who have gone before us and have paved the way for our incredible economic success. It was with keen foresight that our predecessors headed off a dangerous activity that was threatening our very way of life. Heated speeches were made across the country demanding that this traitorous anti-American behavior be confronted. Riotous crowds on the verge of taking the law into their own hands became commonplace. The cry went out across this great land: "Stop recycling, before recycling stops us."

Recycling isn't a new concept. Every kid in America used to hunt pop bottles. I say "hunt," because littering isn't a new concept either. Searching along the roadsides and down the alleys would net two cents for each bottle found. A short afternoon's work in virgin territory could take a kid to the movies. This reprocessing business became a source of irritation for the miners who worked in the pop bottle mines. These people were rightfully irritated over losing overtime pay. The union leaders took their heated grievance to the last "elect me for growth" politician and said, "Our people are working their rear ends off in those hot dirty pop bottle mines trying to assure gold in the Consumer Olympics, and at the same time, these miserable kids are running around like a bunch of little Labrador Retrievers fetching the old ones back. DO SOMETHING!"

This forceful request to curb recycling, fortunately occurred during an election year, and an important American innovation was born out of necessity (the necessity of staying in office). The "non-returnable bottle" was the subject of great fanfare and gained immediate acceptability by the unions. What this dazzling move had done for the pop bottle miners didn't go unnoticed by the other unions, who had also secured votes for the "elect me for growth" guy.

Pressure was brought to bear on the politicians, as in, "We are considering a concentrated and unified effort of epic proportion that could well prove counter to your aspirations of continual service in your present line of employment. Such an effort will be launched, should we not see some diligent activity on your part that directly influences the remuneration that we are receiving as compensation for our conscientious efforts directed at taking Tin in this years Consumer Olympics." I'll translate that. "We want some of what the pop bottle miners got or you'll be on the extended unemployment list."

This motivational spiel is said to be the stimulus which prompted the "non-returnable" revolution to give way to yet another important era, referred to as the "non-returnable, non-reusable period." This would eventually lead to the "non-sustainable era," but not yet. Thankfully at this point, the Carpenter's Union had not reached full strength and the "non-reusable home" bill failed by a slim margin. America was on the move again, with our national economy running like a Timex, "It takes a lickin' and keeps on tickin'."

You can see how the future was shaping up to look pretty darn good. Moving into the non-reusable, non-returnable era had spawned an entire new industry dubbed the Giant Landfill Business. Thousands of additional American workers were employed in this marvelous and seemingly endless new opportunity. "You call, we haul." Whoa, buddy, we're cookin' on the front burner now.

You have probably noticed that the spirit of this writing is based on the ups and downs of our economy since inception, coupled with the proven scientific concept, "If it appears that every thing is going right, you've probably overlooked something." These continual trials and tribulations were due in large part to the fact that the original foundation for our economy was built on a swamp which requires the necessity of jacking it up now and again.

The chief problem that seemed to threaten the future of the now-dynamic Giant Landfill Business was the very real potential of running out of holes and canyons to act as giant receptacles. Not to worry, American ingenuity and the best government that money could buy found a way. I didn't say a *good* way. Politicians and corporate heads in coastal states that didn't border the Grand Canyon were charged with finding a viable solution to the inevitable Giant Landfill depository bottleneck. Once again, the brightest of the bright came together. A new slogan emerged as a result of their genius: "You hail, we sail." A frequent comment heard from retired politicians of that era is, "I don't know what happened to the ocean, it was alright when I left." These people were nothing short of masterminds.

Okay, we were back on track with the pedal to the metal, coasting downhill with the transmission in neutral (referred to as "Georgia Overdrive"). Everything was wonderful, what could possibly stop it now? Have you ever heard the statement, "Don't look back now, but I think there's something gaining on us"? In this instance, it was a full-sized locomotive disguised as a little overlooked sector of the economy known as Durable Goods.

Durable goods are the category of manufactured products that is defined in economic terms as "lasting far too long" or "unlike computers." Products whose life expectancy was longer than the gestation period of a guinea pig began showing up for what they really were, over-engineered. This is the sector of our economy that includes housing, autos, tractors, machinery, and brick outhouses. A slogan attributed to the latter is, "Built like a brick outhouse," and is still used today for describing objects that appear to have lasting qualities. While lasting qualities may

be desirable in some instances, American-manufactured products weren't one of them.

Here's the rub: durable goods have an extended useful lifetime, workers don't. Not good. A house can last for more than
100 years, a car 20 years, tractors and machinery 30 years, and
the jury is still out on brick outhouses. So what if population
growth, and consequently consumption, were to get a little on
the slow side? Even with Earl cranking out money, eventually
everyone who needed or desired any category of durable goods
would have them (the term for this condition is "market saturation"). Is there no end to the problems? No, there isn't.

Product demand for the manufacturer/builder at the point
that market saturation occurs becomes a little sluggish. When
industry remains a little sluggish for an extended period of
time, say an hour and a half... hold that thought a moment,
this is a great time for a pop quiz. Who knows what happens
next? Yell it right out. Who said "extended unemployment"?
Was that you, Alan? Mr. Greenspan is right on target. Without brisk population growth, demand for durable goods would
slow and massive layoffs would take place with little chance of
the non-durable worker ever returning to work. Oh, my aching
head. That can't be good.

The horrific discovery that durable goods were durable was
made in an off-election year. Even under threat, incumbent
politicians have low incentive levels between elections to do
anything, let alone deal with your problems. (Problems during
election year are *jointly shared* problems, while problems between elections are *your* problems.) The current need for a new
dragon slayer would have to come from the private sector.

Thankfully, poor dividends and falling stock prices have the
same effect on CEOs that a failing economy has on politicians:
they get kicked to the curb. The thought of not being referred
to as "Big Guy," and quite possibly not being referred to at all,
combined with the very real possibility of losing the lease on
the Caddy, gave Big Business heads the necessary incentive to
take on the most fearsome dragon, armed with little more than
a pocket knife.

Credit for the profound utterance that resolved this dreadful situation is given to a night janitor who, in seeing a tired and beaten executive team with heads in hands around a conference table, asked, "What are you guys doing here so late?" One of the executives whined, "Trying to deal with the total failure of our products to experience premature malfunctions." "What the heck does that mean?" the janitor asked. "THEY AREN'T BREAKING!" the executive screamed. A little perplexed, the janitor pushed his broom on down the hall muttering, "If it ain't broke, don't fix it." "THAT'S IT!" screamed the executive as he leaped out of his chair, inadvertently slitting his Armani suit jacket with his new pocket knife. "IF IT'S NOT BROKE, FIX IT SO IT WILL BREAK!" This moment has gone down in history as the origin of one of the most important industrial concepts ever conceived: designed obsolescence. They couldn't have hardly called it "designed to fail," could they? And the rest, as they say, is history.

The first corporations to step up to the plate in an effort to forward this incredible concept were General Motors and Ford, who in 1971 introduced the Chevy Vega and the Ford Pinto — America's first disposable automobiles. The notion was ingenious. With proper maintenance, either of these cars could last as long as three months. The concept was pure intellect at work; the timing, however, proved poor at best. These cars were approximately the size of the trunk space of the then-popular Cadillac and Lincoln. That meant that most potential buyers for these new American wonders were those who were already driving Japanese imports.

The Japanese were still a little peeved about the whole atomic bomb thing and were making their second assault on America by importing cars that would continue to run after being rolled down Mt. Everest. This did not bid well for either of the new U.S.-made disposable cars and they were short lived. Both would, almost certainly, have lasted an even shorter period had consumer reports for the Pinto and Vega not been banned from publication due to the possibility of children reading profane material. The Pinto and Vega enjoyed little success while Toyota captured America without firing a shot.

Next up to bat to solve the durable goods woes was the housing industry, which was determined not to be outdone by General Motors and Ford. With unwavering resolve that disposable housing was an idea whose time had come, they pressed forward. Armed with the confidence that shipping an entire house from Japan wasn't an immediate threat, in the early 1970s the weakening housing industry quickly rolled out their new products, literally. Industry marketing gurus created a new and readily acceptable class of living space. History was made; the classic and stylish Mobile Home was born. Overnight, the term "House Trailer" was transformed to Mobile Home, and Trailer Parks became known as Mobile Home Communities. Once again, the housing industry was on a roll. Well, at least on wheels.

The term "Mobile" was not limited to the method of delivery for America's first disposable homes. In areas such as Florida and Oklahoma, it was not uncommon for an entire Mobile Home Community to relocate without the homeowner's knowledge. Had Orville and Wilbur Wright had the luxury of witnessing the flight characteristics of modern mobile homes during both tornados and hurricanes prior to constructing the Wright Flyer, aircraft design might have been far different today.

Bearing witness to the fact that some mobile home models displayed superior flight performance to that of a Boeing 747, mobile home builders became extremely concerned about marketing in problematic areas. Placing mobile homes in some geographical regions of the United States incurred extreme risk to the new disposable home industry; it could be years before a storm blew them away. This oversight was corrected and the majority of mobile homes sold to this day are required to be placed in known hurricane, flood, and tornado-prone locales. To validate the brilliance of this requirement, the Mobile Home industry is flourishing, due to thousands of orders being placed by FEMA (**F**ast **E**asy **M**oney **A**gency) to replace housing in the flood and hurricane-ravaged regions of this country.

The disposable housing industry was a winner of epic proportion. The shift of the housing sector from "durable" to "consumer" goods paved the way for America to reign supreme at the Consumer Olympics for years to come. Several other sectors of the economy ultimately benefited from the brilliance of the new housing industry, not the least of which was oil and gas. The oil and gas gang were taking some shots to the bottom line as a result of those idiots who insisted on driving those ridiculous fuel-efficient Japanese cars. Remember, this wasn't election year, and the possibility of a total ban against the Japanese auto industry seemed remote.

Therefore, seeing an unexpected opportunity in an emerging market, the oil and gas companies offered to give the Mobile Home Industry assistance in the way of providing design and development. The oil companies recruited the engineers that had designed the Pinto and Vega who, due to their current employment status, were readily available. Who better to design this new product than engineers with past experience with products having metal exteriors and wheels? This collaboration was a match made in heaven. In exchange for help at no charge, the oil companies had been granted a seemingly strange concession, which required a minimum of 25% of all new mobile home production to be placed in areas where the average daytime temperature was conducive to raising penguins.

The Vega and Pinto engineers were charged with developing a roof and exterior-wall model that would display the same insulating qualities as a car door, just not as sturdy. The car engineers displayed magnificent aptitude and, on their own merit, additionally introduced the toasty aluminum frame single-pane window, similar to that in a car door. The final design was complete with full, two-inch insulated walls, generous 120-thousandths thick metal siding, and four-ply tires. When the year-end sales reports for new mobile homes came in, there wasn't a dry eye in the house. This was a proud day for American industry. Oil and gas stocks were going through the roof with the news that the annual gas consumption of a single northern Mobile Home Community was equal to that of Rhode Island. I bow to superior intellect.

It is here that I want to point out a very important but little known scientific fact of my own finding. The actual cause for global warming is not from power plant emissions, it's from mobile home emissions. The heat being lost through the walls and roofs of the larger northern Mobile Home Communities is said to have kept the geese from flying south. This finding seems to dispel the lifelong notion that my dad embraced — that we couldn't heat the whole outdoors by holding the door open.

I'm confident that you never expected to learn the true cause of global warming from such an unlikely source. It's been said that I have a scientific mind. My medical physician, ol' Doc Wheezer, has on more than one occasion mentioned that my mind was of interest to science. He said that lending my mind to science would be of great service. His actual words were, "Since you're not using it anyway, it would be great if you were to lend your mind to science."

The auto industry did ultimately enter into a lucrative three-way partnership with the oil companies and the mobile home gang. What was originally determined to be a complete failure for developing a self-propelled delivery system for new mobile homes became a monstrous new spin-off industry, dubbed the "Motor Home." Travel the U.S.A and never leave home! The Motor Home was America's claim to another envious first, the disposable vacation property. The Motor Home had also opened the door to sell only slightly altered "mobile" homes to a more affluent populace. The original class "A" mobile home was capable of obtaining fuel economy approaching two miles per gallon and had slightly less resale value than a boat. It was perfect. The year that the big motor homes hit the market, several countries boycotted the Consumer Olympics, citing unfair competition and the suspicion that the American public was on drugs.

The finance companies did have to overcome some unforeseen difficulties. Repossession became a definite bummer on those occasions where neither the non-paying owner nor the house was living at the registered address. Yet, considering the whole, pop bottles are one thing, but an entire disposable house? Let's give credit where credit is due.

America's economic engine was hitting on all cylinders. The "elect me for growth" crowd was assured another term and all of our future problems were solved. Oh yes, the pigs are fed and ready for flight.

ECONOMICS 301, SHARING THE WEALTH

AT THE END OF CHAPTER 2, the seemingly (emphasis on "seemingly") endless consumption made possible by broadening disposables to include housing and transportation had America steaming full speed ahead. The giant landfill business was getting nothing but better, and the Great American Dream seemed to be within reach of nearly every American. Well, maybe not.

I saw most of you glancing back just then to see what was gaining on us this time. I won't hold you in suspense: the issue was money — again. Or should I say, a lack thereof. Don't get me wrong, throwing away cars and houses every few years was definitely the answer for keeping everyone working for the time being. The problem came with the fact that the payments now lasted considerably longer than the products.

Bankers and salespeople call this condition being "upside down." This state is also defined as "owing a greater amount of money than the encumbered collateral can be resold for, when offered in an arm's length transaction." For the rest of us, that is simply to say that we owe more than it's worth. Bankers do have a way with words.

Everyone had been so overjoyed with all the newfound wealth created by disposable houses and cars that this little hitch in the payment plan had come as somewhat of a shocker to the financial community. This surprise to the bankers was no surprise at all for the consumers. Anyone who had bought a car since 1910 had been "upside down" two minutes after leaving the dealership. The speed with which depreciation occurs on the average American automobile would make a cheetah appear to be backing up.

Being "upside down" is bad for everyone concerned. Once a person gets upside down, the bank and the salespeople take them off their Christmas card list. Once *off* the card list, the consumer is placed *on* the bank's "it ain't gonna happen" list. This ultimately reduces the number of people qualified to borrow money for the sole purpose of purchasing more stuff, and it's all downhill from there. The situation is starting to look familiar, isn't it? As a result, extended unemployment and reduced tax collection mandate going out to the swamp and jacking up the foundation of the economy, one more time.

When the above scenario continues to unfold, there are two things that can be done to avoid the most horrible of situations from occurring (CEOs and politicians being unemployed).You have often heard that nothing changes in America until our backs are against the wall. That seems to be true, but something happens a whole lot sooner when CEO's and politician's backs are against the wall.

I stated that there are *two* things that could be done to correct this latest shortfall in consumer spending. One is to raise everyone's wages in order to provide greater expendable income, and thus infuse greater capital into the sluggish economy. This first method is based on the "if they have it, they'll spend it" theory. Government tax collection is living proof that this is not a theory, but a constant. The second manner of picking up the pace in a down economy is to involve large numbers of new consumers.

Raising everyone's wages seems like a good idea on the surface, and since most lawmakers are superficial (not to be confused with Super-Official), it has become the most common manner of introducing a quick fix. It is also the easiest fix, and once it is mentioned to lawmakers that a particular plan is the fastest and easiest way out, there is no need to confuse the issue with "better" and "more sensible."

It also doesn't hurt that raising wages is heavily backed by the vote-getting labor unions. Not to mention that nearly everyone loves a raise. "Hold on here," you say. "Government isn't in a position to directly increase wages to private business employees." Very perceptive you are. But, remember, Earl and the Fed can be very persuasive, and also remember that private business is also looking for a way to get out of this latest financial jamb. Let's just say that they are all willing participants.

To raise wages, all we need now is more money in order to pay...well, more money. You will recall back in Chapter 2 that Earl had been hired to run the Mint and the Bureau of Engraving and Printing. Earl had now been joined by his extended family, including Earl Junior. "More" is what America was built on. The saying, "There's more where that came from," originated at the Bureau of Engraving and Printing.

I'm not purposely picking on these politicians, but I can't help it; there was another small problem on the horizon, which is often the case when the criterion for solving the original problem was "what's fastest and easiest?" I didn't really want to get into this part of our discussion so early, because it's ugly and we were starting to have such a good time. However, I suppose we may as well deal with it, as it's going to become a very familiar term for our remaining chat. When Earl prints a lot more money and passes it around for higher wages, it results in a brand new problem, called "inflation."

Who can tell us what the effects of inflation are? I see a hand go up right in the front. Go ahead, Mr. Carter. Yes, a sufficient amount of inflation does have the same effect as depression and necessitates moving out of the White House. I was actually thinking more about the effects that inflation has on the general citizenry. Does anyone else have an opinion about inflation? Way in the back, the Speaker of the House has an idea. For those of you who couldn't hear what the Speaker said, he stated that inflation is what the chauffer does to a low tire on the limo. And you wonder how we got to this point!

Actually, the low tire concept is not that far from the truth. When a tire gets low, you pump in air. When the economy gets low, you pump in money. From the standpoint of the government, both hot air and money are free (at least *they* aren't the ones who are going to pay it back). Be it a tire or the economy, the fact that it was running low would alert a normal person to the very real possibility that there may be a greater underlying problem at play. Even the dimmest person would suspect that the absence of air in a tire could potentially be the result of a leak. Therefore, fixing the leak, rather than dealing with the symptom of low air, would seem a better alternative. This is where the similarities between the dimmest person and those running our country cease.

To begin with, dealing with the problem rather than the symptom is reasonable, which in itself totally eliminates the thought process of government and Big Business. But there is a far greater reason why politicians and Big Business don't fix the actual problem associated with this latest financial shortfall: it's difficult.

Difficult, in this case, may be the granddaddy of all understatements. Telling 295 million people that the economy which they depend on for frivolous items such as food, shelter, and clothing is no longer viable, is difficult. There are some statements that don't roll off the tongue all that well. This is the epitome of the adage, "Don't shoot the messenger." Fat chance. So that being said, the only question that our fearless leaders have is, "What is the fastest and easiest way out of this mess?" *If stupidity got us into this mess, then why can't it get us out?* — Will Rogers

Inflation is without a doubt the unheralded king of temporary fixes for a perpetual-growth based economy such as our own. The fact that inflation and illusion both start with "I" is not the only similarity. We'll get to that later, as there is a limit to the extent of bad news that a person can absorb in one sitting. The temporary good news (temporary is better than no good news at all) is that just about the time it appeared that every consumer in America was down for the count, tapped out, upside down, off the Christmas card list, and beyond revival, Earl put three of his cousins on second shift and passed out money like life jackets on a sinking ship.

I saved the best news of all for last. The increase in the National Debt for all the free money that Earl was printing was put on the tab for the kids to pay. We brought them into this world and we can take 'em out. After all, we worked hard and deserve a disposable vacation property. "AH HAH! So we *can* have our cake and *eat* it too," I hear someone say. In this case, yes, you can — temporarily. Isn't America grand?

Once wages are increased and the consumers are back on the Christmas card list at the bank, business begins heating up across the country. The increased wages result in increased consumption and the problem is solved. Nah, it's not really solved — I was just kidding. Granted, the production department is now happy as a clam. But the accounting department is pulling their hair out. In America we like to share our problems so that the burden for keeping the show on the road is not always on the same people. So as not to rain on the parade of the now-ecstatic people in the production department, we'll move the problem over to the accountants.

Accounting people are cranky. When business is good and the company is making lots of money, the CEO is responsible. When business is bad and the company is losing lots of money, accounting is responsible. This is often referred to as a "no win" position. Wait staff in restaurants often find themselves in this same conundrum. When diners enjoy their meal, they say, "My compliments to the chef," and they leave a nice tip. When they don't enjoy their meal, they say, "There is gristle in my filet mignon and it wasn't cooked properly. This is the worst meal I have ever eaten in my life, and I'm never coming back into this establishment as long as I live." After which they storm out the door. You will notice that the chef was not mentioned in the latter example. The waitperson is making $1.85 per hour, has no say whatsoever regarding the food preparation, and a tip under these circumstances doesn't look good. Wait staff are cranky also.

Getting back to our accounting department's problem, remember that the production department is happy because everyone got a raise and work is coming in hand over fist. So what's the problem? Accounting has come to the realization that the recent raise in wages is costing the company more money on payday (accounting people are trained to pick up on these things). Accounting also came to the conclusion that paying out more money for labor is cutting into the profits and the bottom line is somewhat anemic. Accounting takes this bit of news down the hallway to the CEO, who blames accounting for not presenting better numbers. A meeting of the board of directors is called immediately, but can't be held for six weeks due to conflicting schedules and tee times.

Once the board gathers and the facts are presented, the great minds begin to meld together to form a viable solution. When the idea of hiring new accounting people with better numbers fails to gain traction, one of the brighter board members suggests raising prices on the company's manufactured products in order to counteract the losses incurred from paying higher wages. Now *there* is a concept. Once the higher prices have a positive effect on the bottom line, the accounting people take the good news to the CEO, who in turn takes full credit for the turnaround and gets a $5 million bonus from the board of directors. The CEO and the board schedule a retreat in Honolulu to reflect on their brilliance, and the accounting people go back to their offices and get crankier.

The most amazing part about this whole ridiculous chain of events is that I'm not making it up! Every company has to raise wages to keep their help from going over to the competition, who what? That's right — raised wages. And business *appears* to be so good that everyone is expanding and continually trying to hire their competitor's employees for the now higher wages. The dog is in full pursuit of this tail.

Once every company has been forced to raise wages, and consequently raise prices, the cost of goods rises to the level of the new wages being paid. Alright, take an absolutely wild stab at what happens next? I am so proud of you all for paying such admirable attention; you nailed it right on the head. What the heck, it was fast and easy; we'll just repeat the process. Truth is stranger than fiction.

But of course, there is a backlash. Do you remember those boring stories that your grandparents used to tell? They went sort of like this: "Why, I remember when I was a kid, we walked ten miles uphill in two feet of snow with no shoes just to go to the picture show. We only had 25 cents, which would pay admission to the show and buy a soda. When we were your folk's age, gas only cost 12 cents per gallon and we bought a house for $2,500 with indoor plumbing. I don't know what this world is coming to with people paying $1.50 for a bottle of free water and $5.00 for a cup of 25-cent coffee." Your grandparents had experienced a little inflation in their lives and could see that it wasn't working out all that great, at least not for them. But then again, they had the option of planning for prices to increase by 100% over three years, so poor planning is their tough luck. At least that's what they say in Washington D.C.

In economics, inflation is described as "an increase in the general level of prices of a given kind in a given currency." *General* inflation is descibed as "a fall in the purchasing power of money within an economy." What they are trying to say is that a buck doesn't go as far as it used to. So if inflation is bad, why do we experience constant inflation? Go back to the part where our government officials have to tell the good citizens that things aren't really working out the way that they would have liked for them to, and that Spam will soon be classified as a gourmet meal. Looking at it like that, what harm could a little inflation do?

Another definition of inflation stated by *FUTURECASTS* on-line magazine is: "Monetary inflation is a kind of tax with which government — by expanding the money supply — transfers wealth from its people to itself. It also results in the transfer of enormous amounts of wealth from the hands of ordinary people to the hands of those speculators shrewd enough to take advantage of the price volatility inflation causes in the markets."

My hat goes off to *FUTURECASTS* for stating the real effects of inflation so eloquently! Now we're getting somewhere. With more money in circulation and higher wages being paid for purchasing higher priced goods and services, more taxes can be collected. The latter part about the "shrewd speculators" is aimed at those having insider trading information and who know when to sell just before the price collapses on the unsuspecting "ordinary people." This occurs all day, every day, but so far only Martha Stewart had to do time for it.

By this point, you may suspect that there are some additional advantages to both the government and our fragile economy by maintaining a brisk level of inflation. I congratulate you on observing correctly. The major positive effect that inflation provides for government occurs in the "asset value to debt ratio" of our National Debt. It should be recognized that both the State's and Federal Government's most valuable asset is none other than the American taxpayers, therefore, the better the good ol' taxpayers are doing (regardless of what it takes to make it appear that way), the better the benefits for Congressional retirement.

I know that it's hard to decipher all the mumbo jumbo that the government puts out about the Fed. Such subjects as discount rates, selling treasury notes and bonds in relation to printing money, comparing yield curves on short-term and long-term instruments, and if the yield curve inverts it's a sign of a bad thing, and yada yada yada. I want to once more reduce these legions of rules and regulations to a simple statement. They have Earl, and they have you. Earl prints it, you pay it back. If you can't pay it back, your kids and grandkids pay it back. Now isn't that a whole lot easier to understand?

So, this is really a matter of how you are doing. Your government needs you (and you thought it was the other way around). Here's an example. Let's pretend that you bought a home 20 years ago for $50,000. Today the value of that home is $200,000. You then have equity of $150,000, less any amount that you may have paid toward principle, so add another $39.00. You made improvements, like raking the yard and painting the house, so add those improvements, less a discount on the paint job due to your brother-in-law helping you. That comes to another $29.95. All together you have equity of $150,068.95.

So how can your house be more valuable now than it was 20 years ago, when today it needs new plumbing, new windows, a new roof, a new furnace, new carpets, and a professional painter to fix your brother-in-laws paint job? One word — inflation. This wonderful system allows you, the lucky home owner, to borrow four times more money on your current home than you paid for it. The real rise in price isn't that the house is worth more; it's that your money is worth less. A lot less. That isn't the end of the good news. Being the outstanding registered taxpayer that you are, this increase in your new-found inflated wealth is transferred to the very Federal Government that serves you so well. The government can now borrow more money to add to the National Debt, while maintaining an attractive asset-value to debt-ratio due to your hard work and a little culinary accounting. Figures don't lie, but liars figure.

It looks like everyone is winning with the inflation thing, which is creating more money to spend, and more stuff to spend it on. No doubt, inflation keeps the show on the road, so to speak. But no different than in Las Vegas, where there are winners, there are losers. Inflation has a couple of drawbacks, actually *hundreds* of drawbacks, but if we dwell on only a few subjects, we won't ever get to the end of this discussion. We will limit the debate of drawbacks to two *minor* issues, and one *major* issue, one real major issue of significant importance to forming the big picture — a picture that you *for sure* don't want to be starring in.

The first minor drawback of inflation is the effect that it has on savings. Americans are said to have the lowest savings rate of any industrialized nation in the world. The government pretends that they don't know why this occurs, and blame the citizens for being fiscally irresponsible. In reality, they know *exactly* why Americans have low savings rates, because that is *exactly* how the system is designed. Let me show you. I hate these complex math problems, so I've once more simplified the equation by applying my patented "Mikemathics." Say you put $1,200 in savings on January 1 of the current year, and let's also say you have a better-than-average banker and are collecting a whopping 2% interest. At the end of one year, you will have amassed the unbelievable sum of $24.00 in interest, or a total of $1,224 in your savings account.

Let's also say that government inflation figures show that inflation grew by 3% for the year (6% in reality, but then we don't live in reality, we live in America, home of Fantasyland).

Taking the reported inflation into account, the purchasing power of your $1,224 would be reduced by 3%, or would be equal to $1,187.28. This is not the end of the good news. The I.R.S. realizes that you are benefiting from this exorbitant interest windfall, and, therefore, your bank is going to send you a statement indicating that you made $24.00 in interest, which must be added to your taxable income.

Just for grins, let's say that you are in the lower tax bracket of 15% and have a state income tax of 5%, in which case your $24 would now be subject to a 20% tax, or $4.80. (When you make the big bucks, you gotta pay up). The result is that the $1,200 that you originally invested in savings, after collecting interest, and now paying taxes, has $1,182.48 in after-inflation purchasing power, or $17.52 less than you started with! Now if that doesn't make you want to save money, what would? The greatest fear of all government officials is that the majority of the voters will all wake up on the same morning.

The second *minor* drawback that I talked about is the effect that inflation has on people who are on fixed incomes (we touched on this earlier). After people retire, in most instances, the only raise they get is a raise in what it costs them to live. Retirement income and social security are not nearly as inflationary as food, shelter, clothing, and Starbucks coffee. So, when inflation forces prices up on rents, groceries, medical treatment, utilities, insurance, fuel, and other frivolous expenditures, those on fixed incomes don't fare so well — also termed as, "being between a rock and hard place." For this group of people, inflation is a real bummer. If our politicians and CEOs had the same concern for the bulk of the American people that they do for their own welfare, I seriously doubt that purposely induced inflation would ever be a consideration.

Remember earlier in the chapter when I said that the good news was that your kids were going to have to pay the interest on all the inflated money and national debt? And, that you could keep your cake and eat it too — temporarily? The temporary part is the bummer. To fully benefit from inflationary costs not outrunning your retirement requires that your retirement be..., let's say, brief. If you want to dance to the music, you have to pay the fiddler.

We have covered the two *minor* side effects of inflation that I promised to tell you about. I did say that we would discuss one *major* drawback, as if the minor matters are not irritating enough. I also stated earlier in the chapter that there were two ways out of our latest predicament. One was induced inflation, which we discussed. The other was adding additional consumers to the mix, which we most definitely need to discuss. Adding additional consumers and the major drawback to inflation (at least in the United States) are closely connected and worthy of devoting the next chapter to. As Admiral, David G. Farragut said, *"Damn the torpedoes! Full speed ahead."*

CHAPTER 4

ECONOMICS 401, A BRAND NEW FIX

WE LEFT CHAPTER 3 while discussing (and now cussing) the economic cure-all elixir of inflation. As we saw, there are a few kinks that need to be worked out of that plan. Older people need to quit whining about not having a livable income, and the current kids and grandkids need to buck up and pay the bill. After all, there are 78 *million* baby boomers counting on them to fund their retirement.

"So if doing in the old people and the kids are the *minor* issues, what in the world is the *major* issue?" I knew you were going to ask. I'll give you three guesses and the first two don't count. If you are a baby boomer who thought you might just sit this entire game out, suit up, Champ, you're going in. Don't get too nervous just yet, because for now, you can continue to sit on the bench. The first string isn't quite played out, and, luckily, we just came up with an entire batch of new recruits. Keep in shape though; you're definitely going to be called on.

The second possibility that we talked about for reviving a less-than-brisk economy, other than paying everyone more wages, was to come up with a new group of additional Wal-Mart shoppers. So where do additional shoppers come from when everyone in America is spending as fast as they can? Remember when we talked earlier about immigration? It is a common misnomer that I.N.S. is an acronym for Immigration and Naturalization Services. It actually stands for **I**nstant **N**ecessary **S**hoppers.

Albert Einstein said, "Make everything as simple as possible, but not simpler." You may have observed that I am somewhat overqualified in the simple department. That being said, here's my slant on why America has the constant requirement for additional immigration, legal or illegal: *they have to come, they're the main attraction in this crazy sideshow that we refer to as "our economy."*

I do apologize for having to continually go back to historical illustrations, but there is just no other way to connect the dots. Early on in the United States, we got along fine practicing what we call "domestic expansion." In other words, there was still a lot of vacant land that we could take away from the Indians and resell. Even the lands that were acquired by fair trade, such as the $24.00 in trinkets that was exchanged for Long Island, worked out well in the resale market. Looking at Long Island today, the Indians probably got the long end of the stick.

In the early colonial days, Americans couldn't rely heavily on foreign nations for trade because it took the majority of a person's life to sail across the ocean. Communication also posed a problem (Alexander Graham Bell and the Wright Brothers came later). By the time an order reached Europe and they waited for the check to clear, there was no need for the hair tonic that had been ordered, due to the customer going bald in the interim. Therefore, rather than import the products, it seemed a far superior plan to simply import the actual people who made the products.

This proved easier to accomplish than one may think. When the people who were manufacturing products in Europe got wind that over in the New Americas they didn't have to wear those dumb hats and there were nude Indian beaches, thousands volunteered to go.

You may be thinking that importing these craftsmen would somewhat irritate the European companies, who were now not only losing sales to the New Americas, but were also losing their employees. I can see where you could come to that conclusion, should you not have a background in employment law. The CEOs of European companies were no doubt worried initially about the brain drain that was occurring, and predictably assumed that it would negatively affect the bottom line.

It is said that when you see a person in a bad spot suddenly start to smile, it is because they have thought of someone else to blame. Grinning from ear to ear, one CEO sent the problem down to the people in the accounting and human resources departments to get current financial numbers and set up a potential scapegoat. The accountants unexpectedly came back with good news. Anyone who left the country for new employment would have no claim to their accrued retirement and company benefits.

Acting responsibly on this key information, as you would expect, the CEO canned all the older workers and sent them to the New Americas, whether they wanted to go or not. This clever move saved the company thousands, by allowing the accounting department to rebook future liabilities at lower values. The CEO took all the credit for the new windfall and received a huge bonus from the board of directors. At the same time, the New Americas got the best craftsmen in the world. So everyone was happy. Well...not everyone, the accountants just can't seem to win.

There are lengthy books written by Harvard and Yale economists that go into the most intricate details surrounding the economy that developed in the New Americas as our society evolved. These manuscripts normally begin at a point when the planet was in a molten state and continue for 2,000 pages, while endlessly philosophizing over the minutest detail in a cruel medical experiment aimed at determining whether it is possible to bore a person to death.

Entire chapters in these books (it should be pointed out that a chapter in a Harvard economist's book is somewhat longer than the Amazon River) are devoted to such interesting subjects as the economic history of shipping goods by camel across the Atlantic Ocean. The study begins with the first discovery of camels as a species on the planet, and concludes some 500 pages later with the unexpected result that the camels drowned about five miles west of London. After which it was reasoned that caravans were not practical as a means for transcontinental shipping until such time that further research could determine the cause for the failure — which would require another lengthy study! *I have never let my schooling interfere with my education.* — Mark Twain

All that being said, here is the same story from the King of Simple, and presented in a special study of economics that are blended with common sense and reasoning called "Mikeronomics." I call the economy that our forefathers developed the "Butcher, the Baker, and the Candlestick Maker" era. Each person made something that the other person *needed* and the world went around nicely. If you give good people freedom, natural resources, and get out of their way, they will create commerce. Why? It makes their lives better and easier. Now there's a noble concept, and a 500-page book, all in one paragraph.

America was a big beautiful empty land with vast natural resources and no end in sight to the growth that was possible. You will notice that from inception, that growth was the main ingredient. Everything worked out fine until the point when the Indians were running out of land that the new settlers could take for resale. The Indians by this juncture were, in fact, reversing the trend by pumping oil on the reservations and exacting sweet revenge by taking their money back a quarter at a time in the casinos.

Now that we know why the economic circle went around nicely for everyone in the early years (the Indians were assured that it could have been worse), let's fast-forward to the point where there were more products than people to consume those products, or to the extended unemployment stage of the economic cycle ("cycle" is an economics word for "busted again").

This is where Albert Einstein would have been proud of me. The quantum calculus formulas and resulting calculations required to totally define the correlation between population growth and sustainable commerce in a capitalistic society would look something like this: $z = f(x) = \lim (1/x).\log (1 + h/x) x/h$. We'll do this democratically; who wants to take the quantum calculus approach and who wants to do it Mike's way? Just as I hoped, I'm winning some converts to my system of mathematics (Mikemathics).

Example problem (1):
(a) There are 500 families total in the U.S. who don't have a home, and, at the same time, are qualified to buy a home.

(b) There are 500 contractors in the U.S. who need to build 3 homes each by year-end to stay in business.

Question: How many contractors will be in business by year-end?

If you answered, all of them, because the government would purchase the remaining 1,000 homes for subsidized housing and hurricane relief, you are correct.

Example problem (2):

Question: Same problem as above, but no hurricanes are predicted to occur within the next six months.

If you answered: "It depends on whether this scenario falls on an election year," you have been paying admirable attention and deserve an "A."

Final Exam problem (3):

Question: Same problem as #1, with the exception that it is an election year and no hurricanes are predicted within the next six months.

If you answered: "In order to increase demand for the necessary home consumption in the U.S., the INS will be seeing considerable overtime, while the Border Patrol officers will be given extended paid leave," your keen perception moves you to the head of the class.

Without our ever-increasing immigration, legal or illegal, a system predicated on exponential growth will fail. At some point, we will have to change our model, but don't count on your political representatives to lead the charge.

How about a story problem to put some real emphasis on the subject of oversupply and the accompanying underemployment that results from market saturation?

Story Problem:

(Background) There are two kinds of building contractors in America. The ones that are broke and the ones that are going to be broke. I'll go out on a limb here and say that most contractors assume that once they build a structure, someone will buy it. I say assume, as history has proven that building contractors have no idea that there is a correlation between the sale of buildings and the number of people who want to buy buildings.

Obtaining buyers is left to the real estate professional, who was formerly a building contractor prior to going broke. Real estate people tend to fall into the same two categories of broke or going to be broke, thus the name, Real Estate "Broker."

The real estate professional promises the building contractor that he will show up with buyers from wherever buyers show up from, with the hope of selling the building and collecting a commission without actually investing any money into the construction, as he had so obviously erred in doing during his previous career. You can now see that this process is a very complex and well-organized system which should not be attempted by those who do not wish to broke or Broker.

Problem: If a building contractor builds a large condominium project and uses 500 total workers during the construction (carpenters, electricians, concrete workers, roofers, plumbers, etc.), what will those workers do when the building is finished?

If you answered, "Build another condominium project," you are only partially right and get a "C." If you answered, "Build another condominium project, so long as the last project that they built sold out," you are more correct and get a "B." If you answered, "Oh my God, there is a correlation between selling buildings and people who want to buy buildings," you are at the head of the class.

In an ongoing effort that has spanned decades to assure that there would be a continual stream of buyers to purchase all the new condos that could possibly be built, immigration in the United States has been...let me think of a nice way to say corrupted...okay, "modernized," to the tune of allowing 1.2 million *legal* immigrants to enter annually.

I'm going to test your attention to detail. Do you remember when we talked about those pesky durable goods and how they last way too long? Condos fall into that category. Also, remember how everyone at the beauty shop was against immigration but the government didn't listen? Oh, they were listening all right. That's why they didn't increase *legal* immigration to **1.6** million new consumers per year, which is what it takes to keep the train from coming off the tracks.

Instead, they just let the other necessary 400,000 shoppers sneak in and stay. Don't look at me like that; I didn't have anything to do with it. I just call 'em like I see 'em, and besides, I did the numbers with Mikemathics. The government reports (under severe pressure) that there are somewhere around 11 million illegal immigrants in the United States. They didn't all come in on the same night, and 11 million people aren't all that hard to find if you're looking. But then, who's looking? After all, they need cars and housing, and America needs cheap labor. The picture isn't getting any better is it?

History bears out that increasing immigration has never been a popular subject. Explaining to the good citizens that it is NECESSARY for about 1.6 million new foreign shoppers to join our club every year would, just after the ensuing panic, be political suicide. So, "Let's play dumb" remains the logical choice of our elected Champions.

There are approximately 1.8 million new houses built every year in the U.S. We just discussed the fact that there are approximately 1.6 million legal and illegal immigrants combined, who enter the U.S. each year. I don't want to push you into anything, but do you suppose these two numbers are related? Uh-huh.

Biting at the cover and throwing your book down like that isn't going to help. You gotta cowboy up and stay with me here. Let's take one more Mikemathics quiz.

Question: If 1.2 million immigrants are entering the U.S. legally each year, and 400,000 are entering the U.S. illegally (and staying), and the banks and building contractors are cornering the market on vacant homes, what would *you* do to rectify the situation?

If you said, "I would stand up and tell the American public the truth — that exponential growth is not possible," you had better back off a little on whatever it is you've been drinking. Furthermore, you have no aptitude whatsoever to serve your country as a dedicated elected official. Speaking of lifetime politicians, don't you just love the "dedicated public servant" statement that politicians throw out, with the connotation suggesting personal sacrifice for the good of the country? Why, you couldn't run that lot off with an electric cattle prod.

Getting back to our quiz, if you said, "I'd lie like a rug and suggest that NAFTA would be a nice thing to do for Canada and Mexico, and furthermore, would result in a positive effect on American jobs," you have "presidential material" written all over you.

At the point where it became obvious that condo sales were in the toilet to stay, and that even the mention of increased immigration would surely liberate several of those who were currently serving as our lawmakers from their jobs, a special session of Congress was called. Special sessions are like having to work overtime, and Congress people aren't wild about working at all. That's why they're Congress people to begin with: $158,100 per year, and no heavy lifting.

The conversation went something like this: "While none of us *wish* to be here today, it has come to my attention that if we don't find some quick fix that will result in vigorous condo sales, none of us *will* be here after the next election." Had the chair said something such as, "There is a plague in North Africa that is going to kill 30 million people and we just got word that North Korea is attacking China with nuclear weapons," Congress would have said, "You called us all in to special session to tell us THAT!?" But when they heard they might be liberated from serving their country...these folks slid up on the fronts of their chairs and leaned forward.

"I am soliciting suggestions for a quick and easy fix to this horrible slowdown in condo sales. The Chair appeals to the distinguished gentleman from New York." The distinguished gentleman from New York, whose facial expression now resembled that of a deer in the headlights, came up with a save and said, "Mr. Chairman, I yield my time to my esteemed colleague, the notable distinguished gentleman from the great state of Texas." That's what Congress people say when they have no earthly idea what is going on, which is mostly.

The distinguished gentleman from Texas, who was a Republican, said, "Mr. Chairman, I yield my time to the distinguished lady from the great state of California, who knows evvvereeething." (She was a Democrat.) That's what Congress people say when they have no earthly idea what is going on *and* hope to dump the seemingly unsolvable problem on the opposing party. The distinguished lady from California said, "I resent that remark, and therefore yield my time to any of these idiot Republicans who wouldn't recognize a good idea if it bit them on the butt." That's what Congress people say when they can't think of anything else to say.

This cheerful banter went on until such time as they reached the junior Congressperson in the room, who had no one to yield his time to. He said, "Being that we have imported all the physical people that our voting public will tolerate, and being that the word on the street is that several of the brighter citizens are starting to notice that they have 11 million new neighbors who don't speak English, and who all work at night, the cat may be out of the bag." The Chairman now slid forward on his seat and with a discernable expression of concern said, "Is anyone ready for lunch?"

After lunch, the meeting continued with full stomachs and brighter minds (during lunch, the Congress people had conferred with the catering crew). It was first confirmed that no severe hurricanes, tornados, mudslides, or nuclear wars were eminent that could potentially wipe out half the housing in America. So much for plan "A."

The idea was then considered of attacking the Canadians for saying things like "eh" and "you betcha" in an effort to distract the American public from dwelling on vacant condos. That plan was scrapped when several of the Congress people raised concerns over the fact that they had Canadian stocks in their portfolios, and a war could negatively affect dividends. These people are *thinkers*.

The quest for a solution continued around the table with no viable ideas for a resolution surfacing, and ended with the junior Congressperson being put on the spot to come up with something. "The Chair appeals to the distinguished gentleman from Arkansas for a final solution." The distinguished gentleman from Arkansas answered, "That depends on how you define 'final.'" Not being one to be put off, the Chairman pushed the good Congressman for an answer. The young Congressman said, "Okay, let's break this problem down. We need more sales of American goods, but can't import any more people to buy them, and at the same time be re-elected to further dedicated service.

"Earl is on the verge of printing money to a point that inflation could also interfere with our tenure. So what we really need is for more people to buy American products *outside* of our borders." "Absolutely brilliant!" screamed the Chairman. "How do we do that?" Sensing that he was on the right track, the young Congressman answered smugly, "By opening up the borders to Canada and Mexico to free trade." "Brilliant!" screamed the Chairman again. "Is that good?" "No," the Congressman answered, "but it's quick and easy." "Tremendous!" cheered everyone in the room. "Is anyone ready for dinner?"

The end result was NAFTA, which originally stood for North American Free Trade Agreement, but today it has become evident that it is actually an acronym for **N**ot **A**ltogether **F**air **T**o **A**merica. The idea for NAFTA was to break down the trade barriers, do away with the tariffs, level the playing field, and create a huge market for U.S. goods in Canada and Mexico, thus limiting the increasing need for immigration. "Elect me for growth" was still the only way this was going to work, and now it could be done without increasing the domestic population. What a deal! The whole thing looked good on paper.

The adage "if you're not growing, you're dying" is not just a nifty saying, it's the absolute truth in a consumption-based economy. Our capitalist system cannot exist without continual growth. Well, that's not totally true. Our system *can* and *has* existed without growth. It was called the "Great Depression" and it didn't catch on with the voters.

I mentioned that inflation wasn't the worst thing that we needed to discuss; the *cumulative effect* of inflation is the worst thing (more on this in a moment). I also said that there were two ways out of the stalemate that the economy was in, pay more wages or get more shoppers. As we saw, Congress and the rest of the Beltway gang had determined that continually increasing inflation held the very real potential of interrupting their limousine service, as did increased immigration. That left NAFTA, and it did look good on paper...so, why not give it a try? If you have watched the TV news at least once in the past ten years, it shouldn't surprise you that our government had overlooked an important aspect of the new plan (as they could overlook Mount McKinley on a clear day). There was an important element missing from the new NAFTA shoppers that they had chosen — they didn't have any money. At least not the kind of money that it took to buy American products after 70 years of continual inflation-based pricing.

I'll try and set the scene here. Americans had rushed headlong in their short history, burning through money as if there was no end. The advent of fiat currency, coupled with Earl and family, had convinced most Americans that there really *was* no end to the wealth possible (if it seems too good to be true, don't ask why). By the point that it became evident that there were some serious drawbacks to an economy that was based on perpetual growth, (these types of things tend to slip up on people who haven't been paying attention for 120 years or so), inflation had made America, on paper, the wealthiest country in the world. We were keeping time with a Rolex while the rest of the world was wearing a Timex.

At about the same point that our illustrious government officials realized that the average annual income in Mexico wouldn't cover breakfast at Denny's and a one-night stay at Motel 6, they also realized that "open borders" meant...open borders. Get ready all of you baby boomers; you're going in the game.

American industrial leaders, being somewhat brighter than government officials, realized that while they couldn't sell American-made products to the Mexicans, they could certainly move their American-made manufacturing plants to Mexico. Cheaper wages, no fringe benefits, fewer work rules, modest environmental concerns, and no OSHA inspectors at all: sounds like corporate utopia to me. This is where all of you boomers get to be, shall we say, involved. Due to the new NAFTA rules, the American public now had the advantage of purchasing far cheaper foreign-made products, thus saving loads of money. So what's the problem? The problem is that the new cheaper products are the very ones that the American workers used to make before the company that they worked for moved to Mexico. *Reality is merely an illusion, albeit a very persistent one.* — Albert Einstein

American industry was finally able to manufacture products that could successfully compete in the *world* market, so long as they didn't use American labor, pay American taxes, comply with American environmental standards, or...well...do business in America. The playing field was being leveled for the good of the American people. "I'm from the government and I'm here to help."

Mexican workers were earning approximately $1.25 per hour while United Auto Workers, considering their benefits, were earning approximately $1.25 *per minute.* Leveling wages with such extreme differentiation may seem impossible to those of you who have no background in Government Math. Government Math is an area of special study, and has no relationship to Mikemathics. Here's the way it works.

Several government statisticians, assisted by a team of economists from Harvard and Yale Universities, were charged with a lengthy study to determine the extent of wage disparity as it existed between Mexican and American workers. It was found to be conclusive that Mexican workers did, in fact, make $1.25 per hour. It was then determined that thousands of displaced U.S. workers, whose jobs went to Mexico, were making $0.00 per hour, including overtime. The esteemed panel surmised then that Mexican workers make $1.25 per hour *more* than the control group of unemployed U.S. workers that had been used in the study. As a result, to achieve parity between the two groups, the American workers would have to be given a raise

of $1.25 per hour. Since raises are a good thing, this important finding concreted the original notion that NAFTA was actually good for American workers. Say what!! *Statistics are like bikinis. What they reveal is suggestive, but what they conceal is vital.*
— Aaron Levenstein

I can't credit all of the genius that fashioned NAFTA to Congress, it wouldn't be fair. As you will see, they had a little help from our friends, the Italians.

CHAPTER 5

WE COULDN'T HAVE DONE IT WITHOUT THE ITALIANS

TO TRULY UNDERSTAND who the masterminds were that laid the groundwork for this grand plan that we call the Great American Pyramid Scheme — I mean, the Great American Economic Model — we need to take another short stroll down history lane. It would have never been possible without our friends, the Italians.

There are startling similarities between our modern economic model and the Leaning Tower of Pisa. Both were built on poor foundations, and since inception, both have had to be continually propped up. The famous tower's beginning started in 1173. Had it been started in 1776, I would have been convinced that the architects who designed the foundation for America's economic model and that of the famous Leaning Tower were one in the same.

In the first four chapters, we covered some of the fixes necessary to keep our economy from falling down. The Italians have done the same with the tower. Once it was determined that all the other buildings in Pisa weren't leaning, and that the tower really was the culprit, it became necessary to prop it up. Why? Because the tourists show up every year to see the thing lean, not fall over.

It should not surprise you that the tourist's money shows up with them. As late as 1995, and after countless costly fixes, the tower continued to increase its lean to the south. You can't fix a problem without identifying it, and so it was determined that the Leaning Tower's foundation was not the problem, the tower simply wasn't heavy enough on the north side. Now for the fix, and I'm not making this up: they added 830 tons of lead to the north side of the tower to get a few more years of the visiting tourists money before the thing falls completely over. I'm confident that the United States Congress was called in as a consultant.

Since the lean on the tower was originally observed at the time they were building the third story, it seems the lean on our economic model could have been observed by the time it reached the third day of operation. But then, who's observing?

While both our economy and the Italian's tower need constant propping up, there is a subtle difference in importance to keeping both intact. In Italy, 700,000 tourists show up annually to experience the amazement of seeing the tower lean without somehow tipping over. In the United States, 295 million Americans show up annually to live in an economy whose balancing act is far more amazing, and bet their livelihoods that it *won't* tip over. Bad bet.

America also gained much of the basis for our current economic model from another product of Italy, one Carlo "Charles" K. Ponzi. Charles Ponzi is the person after which the villainous "Ponzi scheme" is named. It's worth a look at Ponzi's financial invention to witness the similarities between the U.S. system of economics and Ponzi's grand scam.

For those of you who don't recognize the name "Ponzi," you will definitely recognize his work, and therefore have a greater appreciation for his contribution to our present system of wealth accumulation. Have you ever been approached with a scheme requiring you to shell out money for the unbelievable opportunity to join an incredible new marketing plan, after which you recruit five additional people to join, after which they each get five more people to join, after which you will start receiving enough money in the mail to purchase the county in which you currently reside? If so, you can thank Charles K. Ponzi.

Charles Ponzi arrived in the United States in 1903 as an immigrant from Italy. He tried one scam and then another before he opened his Boston-based Security Exchange Company in 1919. Charles promised a 50% return on any cash investment, to be paid within 90 days. (Is this starting to sound familiar?)

Within months, Ponzi was making people rich and taking in $1,000,000 per week! Everyone involved was living on Easy Street and Got It Made Boulevard. It seemed (certainly to the investors) that there was no wrongdoing on Mr. Ponzi's part. Even under investigation by authorities (on suspicion that Ponzi's system was too good to be true), without public complaint of wrongdoing, there was little evidence to dispel Mr. Ponzi's investment plan as being anything but brilliant.

So where was the money coming from? Easy — from continual *growth* in the number of people who wanted to earn 50% interest in 90 days. You may have noticed that the secret to Ponzi's scheme was continual growth and greed. Uh-huh — *exactly* like our economy. So as long as those providing money today were growing in sufficient numbers to cover the payment for those who had provided money 90 days earlier, this thing worked like a charm.

Many investors were so happy that they would reinvest their money immediately upon payment for another 90 days. In no time, business became so vigorous around the office that Ponzi was repaying in 45 rather than 90 days, therefore doubling the original 90 day return to the investors. It may not surprise you to learn that this acceleration of payments triggered a little human mechanism called "greed," and people were *literally* lined up around the block to bring in their cash (I'm not making any of this up). This wouldn't be the only time that Charles Ponzi would see a long line at his door.

The ecstatic investors didn't care where the money came from, only that it was coming. What's new? Remember what Will Rogers said about corruption? "It's awful hard to get people interested in corruption unless they can get some of it." Will Rogers also said, "I am not so worried about the return on my investment as I am on the return *of* my investment." In Charles Ponzi's case, truer apprehension could never have been considered.

As with all things that seem too good to be true, it was. Elementary math busted up the game. I keep throwing this word *exponentially* around. In mathematics, a quantity that grows exponentially, or geometrically like a pyramid, is one that grows at a rate proportional to its size. Such growth is said to follow an *Exponential Law*. This implies that for any exponentially growing quantity, the larger the quantity gets, the faster it grows — like a snowball that collects more snow with every revolution. For Charles Ponzi that meant that the longer he ran the scheme, the greater the increase required for people showing up each day to drop off cash, as compared to the number of people showing up each day to collect cash. You can hazard a guess at what happened. The line for picking up became somewhat longer than the line for dropping off, and Charles Ponzi did a little time in the "big house."

I suggested that our government stole all of Ponzi's ideas: His invention is the current model for Social Security, Medicare, and our base economic plan. The one subtle difference is that Ponzi went to jail, but our politicians have diplomatic immunity (meaning, they should do time, but won't).

So moving on... "Oh," you ask, "what happened to Charles?" That wasn't the end for Charlie. Nah, after three and a half years he was released on bond, pending an appeal. Charles wisely took this opportunity to relocate. He showed up next in Florida and got into the real estate business. Ponzi promised all of his investors that their initial $10 investment would translate into $5,300,000 in just two years. As you may suspect, Charlie came up a little long on swamp and a little short on cash and was sentenced to a year in the Florida pen. (Charlie had a history of good ideas and poor timing as to when to take the cash and get out of Dodge). The idea, however, apparently had merit; the promise of 100% annual returns remains the primary real estate investment model in Florida today.

Believe it or not, Ponzi made bail on the Florida rap and once more considered relocation a sound personal choice. Texas seemed a good place to get on a boat and go back to Italy. He was arrested when the boat stopped in New Orleans, and consequently went back to the slammer for several years, after which he was deported to Italy. Charles may have gone back to Italy, but his schemes found a home in our society and government forever.

The Ponzi scheme and the more common pyramid scheme are much the same. The primary difference is that with the "Ponzi," there is the impossibility of endless exponential growth, and no product is involved except money. In a pyramid format, there is still the impossibility of endless exponential growth, but there are unlimited products involved that require exponential sales and ever-greater infusion of Earl's inflated money. While neither one works long term, our economic model in the United States is more akin to the pyramid scheme, requiring continual exponential growth, endless consumption of resources, and wheelbarrow loads of money. Both fail due to that pesky old math, Ponzi schemes just fail sooner.

So now what are we going to do? NAFTA isn't working out worth beans. There were two directions that our leaders could have gone at this juncture: tell the American people the truth and build toward a sustainable future, or come up with another cockamamie growth scheme. "So," you ask, "what's the new cockamamie growth scheme?" You are definitely gaining understanding of the process. You aren't going to believe what comes next, so I'm going to tell you a little story to ease us into the next chapter.

There were two guys who had a truck and were selling hay for a living. They would buy the hay for $1.00 per bale, drive to another part of the state and sell it for a $1.00 per bale. After about six months one of the guys said, "I don't think we're making any money." The other replied, "I don't either, we're going to have to get a bigger truck."

CHAPTER 6

MODERN COLONIALISM

WE LEFT THE LAST CHAPTER with the American worker lower than a snake's belly in a rut. NAFTA seemed to be backfiring, regardless of the Government Math claims to the contrary. We also left a couple of guys hauling hay with a seemingly stupid plan for expansion. Whether those guys quit hauling hay and were elected to Congress, or whether Big Business influenced the next move, it was undoubtedly modeled after the hay haulers' business plan. I told you, you weren't going to believe it.

The next special session of Congress surely went something like this. "I call this special session of the United States Congress to order. Let's get started so that we can get out of here before Happy Hour. Our last special session which created NAFTA seems to be experiencing less than desirable results as to the employment status of the American worker. The Chair appeals to the same idiotic distinguished person that got us into this mess for a solution to getting us out." Appealing to the distinguished idiotic Congressperson, rather than naming a particular member, was somewhat confusing and several of the Congress people began speaking in unison.

Once the confusion was cleared up, the culprit who had actually suggested NAFTA spoke up. "Mr. Chairman, the advent of NAFTA, according to our Chief Economist and backed by sound Government Math, has indicated that an increase in pay of $1.25 per hour was in line for our beloved taxpayers. Taking this proven fact into consideration, can you imagine the benefit that our workers would receive if we were to open the borders with countries paying $3.00 per day, such as China and India?" "Stupendous idea!" shouted the Chairman. "And here I didn't even know that we bordered China and India." "Actually, sir, we don't, but ships have been invented since you took office." "What a grand plan. Will it work?" "Well, sir, the large corporations who contributed so generously to your last re-election campaign surely think so." The chairman ended the meeting by saying, "What was I thinking then? Of course it will work." (Re-election.) "Who wants to take the limos to Happy Hour?"

That may not have been exactly how it went, but it's a whole lot closer than you would like to believe. If all the Mexican and Canadian people couldn't get the job done, why not get a bigger truck? I didn't mention the downside of recruiting the Canadians all that much in the last chapter. They didn't have money to purchase American-made products either, but for different reasons. The first is that the warmest place in Canada is dang cold, so they spend an inordinate amount of their money buying heating fuel. The second is that the Canadian government takes even more of the good taxpayer's money than does our own to support, among other things, a socialist health care system. And third, affordability of U.S.-made products is made even more difficult for our Canadian neighbors, whose dollar was worth only 70 cents American at the inception of NAFTA. As the saying goes for most failed projects, "It really did look good on paper."

The new plan unveiled for expanding the incredible benefits demonstrated by NAFTA to the rest of the world was the WTO, or World Trade Organization. There are those who contend that WTO actually stands for **W**ho **T**ook **O**ver? NAFTA had taken effect January 1, 1994, and the original WTO, with its 76 member countries (including the United States and India), became effective one short year later, on January 1, 1995. China didn't actually enter the WTO until December 11, 2001. Thank goodness. We now had a bigger truck — a *lot* bigger.

When I said that NAFTA had demonstrated incredible benefits, I didn't say who had benefited. While it may not have been obvious to the public at large that our economic system was beginning to experience some telltale symptoms of having reached its predictable peak, it certainly hadn't escaped the notice of Big Business. NAFTA had given Big Business a new taste of profits that were reflections of those earned in the good old days. The passage of the WTO propelled Big Business from the good life to the great life. If NAFTA was a VW Bug, the WTO was a Greyhound bus.

Break out the good stuff and let's have a toast. American industry heads began moving their manufacturing plants to exceptionally populous, but equally poor, countries. The result created a phenomenon that hadn't been observed in years — HUGE PROFITS. But what about the American worker? *The incestuous relationship between government and Big Business thrives in the dark.* — Jack Anderson

Have you ever noticed that when something really bad is getting ready to happen to you, that it is normally preceded by rationale supporting the premise that this bad thing is actually going to provide you a benefit? I have read countless reports touting the virtues of the proliferation of the U.S. market with cheap foreign products. The authors of these reports contend that free trade creates jobs by reducing prices. The stated logic is that the savings realized from lower-cost goods will leave more money in the hands of the consumer to spend elsewhere. And that the additional money spent will have the effect of stimulating production and employment. These reports are most often written by those individuals anointed with a PhD in economics, and whose well-rounded backgrounds do not include gainful employment. I'm fearless, and they scare me.

At the time of this writing, General Motors and Ford have announced that they will be closing many U.S. plants. Between these two companies alone, approximately 60,000 hourly and white collar workers will be furloughed. At the same time, Delphi, the nation's largest auto parts manufacturer, has filed for bankruptcy protection and is explaining to their 34,000 hourly workers that the company can no longer compete with foreign rivalry, unless they will accept a 60% pay cut. I would buy a ticket to see an economist personally explain the benefits of foreign competition to these people. Combat pay would be in order. Delphi has 65,000 workers in Mexico and 185,000 workers worldwide. The bankruptcy does not include the plants outside the United States. Surprise, surprise.

I'm not an economist by formal education, a fact for which I will remain eternally grateful. I tend to agree with Will Rogers' wisdom: "An economist's guess is liable to be as good as anybody else's." I'm not even sure of that. Something goes terribly wrong between the time a healthy young mind enters college and that time when they can be referred to as "the good doctor of economics." Never confuse economics with mathematics.

From page one, I've beat up unmercifully on America's plan to continue down the path of consuming our way to utopia. I haven't changed my mind. But, I'm not a guy who cuts and runs at the first sign of trouble either. Unlike most countries in the world, we did, in fact, have a plan. The plan was for the American people to be free, and for the government to get out of their way. This is a little known piece of information to the average university economist. It is of significance to learn that a person can receive a doctorate in the field of economics without so much as cracking an American history book.

The people who settled this country weren't big on living in stick huts and eating grub worms. America wasn't an experiment designed to ascertain the lowest level of existence that a human could attain. Our forefathers had already experienced that lifestyle, and actually shot a few people who wanted to return them to their former standards. It was called the Revolutionary War.

Some years later, those same determined people held a little skirmish that you may remember as the Civil War, against their own countrymen over slavery and the poor treatment of other human beings. I wouldn't put it past some of our current citizenry to take particular offense to the plans that call for lowering living standards in order for the remainder of the world to gain parity. It may be of interest to you that the plan doesn't call for lowering standards for politicians and business executives.

History has proven over and over that pompous people in high places don't want to rile the good citizens too much in a democratic society where those good citizens have inalienable rights and firearms. The standard of living that exists in America is not an accident; it was planned and created *on purpose*! As flawed as it may be, we all need to adjust together for a sustainable future that does NOT include mud huts and grub worms. This is in fact, still America. "Set your goals in concrete, and your plans in sand." We need a different plan — a very different plan.

Now that I have that off my chest, why don't we further examine the theory regarding the wonderful benefits that have been bestowed on us by access to cheap foreign goods?

1. The first claim is that free trade creates jobs: I'm not going to argue with that one, but this type of job creation requires the rigors of relocating. Besides, learning to speak Chinese as a 40 year old is difficult.

2. The second claim is that the consumer will have extra money to spend due to all the savings realized from purchasing cheap goods: This statement is somewhat tougher to dissect, but let's try and work through it with Mikemathics. Unemployment does not normally pay 100% of the wages that a person's past gainful employment provided. Therefore, the cost of Chinese goods would have to be low enough to compensate for the difference between the job that a person used to have, and the unemployment *or reduced wages* which they are now collecting. At the same time, there also needs to be the availability of the promised surplus cash to spur the predicted additional spending, that will in turn create investment and new jobs. Give me a minute to do the math...okay it won't work. *Do not put your faith in what statistics say until you have carefully considered what they do not say.* — William W. Watt

3. The third claim is that open borders are ultimately good for everyone: To this, I would then suggest that we outsource all of the teaching jobs currently held in our Universities. The cost of an education in the United States is becoming, to say the least, punitive to our youth. I believe that there are foreign educators who would gladly accept these positions for far less pay and benefits. Even better, we could close down all government-funded institutions of higher learning in America and use

the savings to send our kids to lower-cost foreign universities. This would accomplish two things: we could level the playing field in the education arena and, at the same time, the kids could get a first-hand view of what their lives are going to be like in the very near future should we fully embrace the current plan to level the global playing field.

What is that you said, professor? You are starting to see this thing a little differently now, and perhaps you were a tad hasty with your original findings? I can see where that could happen.

Do I believe that open borders for trade are a bad thing? Not at all, with the exception that we should have adopted the idea about a hundred years ago. The real problem in a nutshell is that America has pursued a path that has distanced us economically from nearly every nation on earth. That's not to say that a few Kings, Dictators, and Warlords don't imitate our standards, but by and large, no regular folks can. In the past we have counted on domestic expansion, high import duties, and countless quick fixes to policy to keep the show on the road. My wise old dad used to say, "Let's get the rules straight before we start the game." NAFTA and the WTO have drastically changed the rules long after the game began.

So how does American labor compete with foreign workers? Some of who *literally* earn 3% of that of the average American employee? Put simply, they don't. The good news is, however, that according to our government and the economists, there are thousands of new jobs in America just waiting to be had. There are a few minor details that those economists and government officials forgot to give you, but by now, you know that I will gladly provide that information.

On the surface this departure from our original domestic expansion model may appear to have some merit. (The poorer a person's math skills, the more merit they may see.) Yet, my belief is that for the practice of globalization to have ever had any positive effect on America's masses, such an effort would have had to begun long ago. Our forefathers (and foremothers — otherwise we wouldn't be here) would have had to establish laws aimed at effectively controlling development and commerce to levels that would insure continual parity among trading partners. Of course, being a Republic, that would have required a vote of the people. Here is a sample of that proposition on the election ballot:

"Shall the people of the United States of America elect to live in mud huts and eat grub worms in order to establish parity with those of future trading partners who are projected to materialize in 200 years or so?"

Bill Clinton couldn't have sold that one, and he sold NAFTA and the WTO in back-to-back years. It is rumored that Mr. Clinton was asked recently, "What *is* the main benefit of NAFTA and the WTO?," to which he answered, "That depends on what the meaning of *is* is." He's still got it.

Given that the citizens would have voted a resounding NO to the former ballot initiative, for better or worse, America moved along and became the largest economic power in the world. Today, rather than suggesting a rational plan for slowing down, we are asked to retreat to a time that this nation passed long ago. I don't believe that such a plan is achievable for many reasons. The *first* is that *Back to the Future* was a fiction movie. The *second* is, that even if it weren't fiction, getting up a group to volunteer to go backwards could prove a daunting task — i.e., impossible. We do actually need to retrieve a few things that we left back in the past, but we'll get to that in a little while.

The real reason that Americans aren't going to go down without a fight is that they don't want to — no more than the good professor wanting to give up his tenure. Of course the professor, Big Business leaders, and the Congress people have never had any intention of actually riding the time machine themselves. After all, someone has to stay behind and look after your best interests.

The concept of making a smooth transition from an agricultural and manufacturing nation to an information and services-based economy seems preposterous to me. If one believes this idea plausible, then one must also assume that steelworkers, autoworkers, machinists, farmers, livestock producers, etc., can seamlessly transition to such employment as systems analysts, computer programmers, and stock brokers. That is one of the bits of information that was omitted from the speech about jobs aplenty for the taking, along with the failure to mention the requirement of two years' experience and a degree in computer science. I can visualize the retraining classes now. "Sir, I believe that if you remove your welding helmet, you could see the computer monitor more clearly."

I also believe that the time necessary for this magnitude of cultural change will simply outdistance America's ability to maintain status quo. (It's trickier than you might think to get the hang of living in a mud hut.) Long before American workers make the necessary transition and prior to our new trading partners reaching an economic level that would make them fair and viable allies, America will be broke.

Not only broke, but left without our manufacturing and farming base. The #1 job in the United States in 2002 (the last year for which I could find census data) was a retail sales clerk! Number 2 was a cashier, and it doesn't get a lot better as the list goes on. So why would we ever agree to NAFTA and the WTO rules if the outcome is so gloomy? **YOU** didn't agree to NAFTA and the WTO. Your esteemed government representatives did, and their personal outlook isn't gloomy at all.

For those people that make up America's most affluent group, this departure from American labor to that of the world's poorest people is certainly not a new idea. The Italians didn't think of this one, the English did. By 1921, the English Empire encompassed 25% of all the people on earth and covered 14.3 million square miles. (The land mass of the United States is 3.5 million square miles.) The English got an early start on acquiring land and subjects in the late 15th century.

The Crown accomplished this by sailing to other countries, jumping off the boat, and saying, "I claim this land for the Queen and I claim these people as the Queen's subjects." It's similar to moving into a furnished apartment. Subjects are citizens who are more or less disposable. They work for the benefit of the Queen and don't get paid. The bright side is that they aren't burdened with filing income taxes. We have to look for the good in everything.

Those who voiced their concerns over the fact that the Queen didn't have any right to claim their land would be shot, and the ones that didn't want to be shot, got to work producing cotton, coffee, tea, spices, cloth, and other desirable and profitable commodities of the time. This method of advancing commerce was dubbed Colonialism, which can be loosely translated from the King's English to mean "stealing and slavery," but Colonialism had a better ring to it.

When they weren't claiming continents and subjects for the Queen, the people who ran the ships would haul all the newly acquired goods back to Europe and sell their bounty at incredible profits, not unlike Exxon-Mobil. All of this new-found wealth allowed English Nobility to assume a life of leisure and implausible excess, without so much as turning a tap. I know, you thought that the Federal Government and Big Business refined that system. Nah, they just took notes. It was from those notes that our system of "Modern Colonialism" was developed.

Modern Colonialism differs from the old English version in several ways. First of all, jumping off of a boat and saying, "I claim this land for King George Bush" falls flat on its face. Think about that for a moment. What if they said "Okay"? That would make the United States responsible for 1.3 billion Chinese who, once they learned our system, would go on unemployment and Social Security Disability. Can you imagine the impact of "no child left behind"? No, no — that won't work; we are having enough problems keeping up with the Louisiana Purchase.

What works best today is to jump off the boat with a bag of Earl's money and say, "I want to employ 100,000 workers for the incredible sum of 15 cents per hour to replace our American work force, who are, like, WAY too costly." I'm going to test your memory again. Do you remember the disposable era that included the non-returnable bottle? Modern Colonialism advances the disposable era to include the non-returnable worker. "Where are we going, and why are we in this handbasket?"

Modern Colonialism has some repercussions. Those repercussions, however, don't negatively impact retiring politicians and won't negatively impact economics professors, unless we adopt my plan for outsourcing higher education. Modern Colonialism mainly affects jobs, which neither of the latter mentioned has. How many of you graduated from high school and college convinced that the world was yours for the taking? Shortly after which you were convinced that you had *been* taken. Your education had little prepared you for what was in store — a real job. And, it got worse when you realized that the only thing at hand for the taking was most of your income, taken by taxes and inflation.

I can't prove this, but I believe that people who become college economics professors somehow secretly find out what life has in store after leaving college; so they don't leave. Politicians have the same secret source, but rather than stay in college, they go into a lifetime of politics to avoid gainful employment altogether. Big Business goes into Modern Colonialism, so that leaves those repercussions that I was talking about for the rest of us to enjoy.

In my mind, there is no possibility for the United States to reinvent ourselves as a nation whose principal employment opportunities lay in the fields of sales clerks, hand laborers (#5, just ahead of waitpersons), and information technicians without dramatically affecting the living standards of Middle America. The basis (domestic expansion) from which Middle America emerged is no longer possible due to the exponential growth required to sustain our present system.

Decades of unrelenting inflation have driven wages and prices in America to levels that preclude the U.S. from competing in many sectors of the world economy. NAFTA and the WTO rules have opened Pandora's Box. Leveling the playing field is far easier to say than do. It has become that time again to apply the unique science of "Government Math" to solve the problem.

Problem: For the sake of simplicity, pretend the world is flat; it's hard to level a sphere. The desired end result of this problem is to level the economic playing field in order to allow every country in the world to become engaged in *fair* trade.

At the present time, there are some minor differences in wage and living conditions for each country involved. These differences are most conspicuous when comparing the basic necessities of food, shelter, and clothing. Some of the nations who require the most leveling (#1 being the United States) have citizens who live in actual homes with indoor plumbing, eat store-bought food on a regular basis, and wear factory-made clothing. In contrast, the people who reside in countries that require fill-dirt for the leveling process, live in naturally occurring homes (called "trees"), eat what ever happens by that can be run down on foot, and wear the outside skin of whatever it was that was successfully run down the week before.

Question: How would you attempt to level this situation?

If your answer is similar to: "I would give the poorer country a score of 0 and the richer country a score of 100 and then divide by 2, arriving at a medium of 50. I would then decrease the rich country's workers' wages by 50% and *increase* the poor countries workers wages by 50%.

"Therefore, if the rich country's workers were earning $15.00 per hour on average, those wages would be reduced by 50% to $7.50, *or* I would lay off 50% of the people reducing them to zero income, which would accomplish the same results.

"Conversely, the poor workers who were earning $0.15 per hour would be given a 50% increase to 22.5 cents per hour, plus overtime at 1.5 times straight pay, and a snack at noon.

"I would then move the rich country's manufacturing plants to the poor country for the benefit of providing jobs for the underprivileged people. This would also achieve the desired end result of creating big old hairy bodacious salaries and benefits for U.S. business leaders and the tyrants...I mean tycoons...on Wall Street.

"I would also give discounts from Foot Locker© to the unemployed workers in the rich country's for purchasing track shoes that could assist them in their new role of running down whatever happened by."

Well done, *well* done. For those of you who answered anywhere near this scenario, you are more than qualified to either serve your country in the political arena, or to move directly into upper management in corporate America.

For those of you who answered, "There is no logical way to accomplish a leveling process under this scenario without destroying Middle America," your track shoe discount coupon should be arriving in the mail any day now.

I believe I heard a little murmur of distain coming from the back of the room. You certainly have a right to be confused. Our government and the talking heads are coloring a somewhat glowing picture for the economy, and certainly the housing market is nothing short of booming. But stick with me for just a little longer and we'll figure out why the good news and the bad news haven't had a head-on collision — just yet.

CHAPTER 7

SMOKE AND MIRRORS

SO HOW IS IT THAT the U.S. government is reporting a white-hot housing industry accompanied by record job growth, and at the same time, yours truly is pointing out the widening crack in the foundation that holds the economy up? Easy — it's all true; the devil's in the details. It's done with smoke and mirrors.

All of the glowing economic news that is being reported is more or less true. *Why* it's true is the critical part of the reporting that seems to lack mention. We talked earlier about the fact that government relies on the poor memories of its citizens regarding past history — say, three weeks ago. Otherwise it could become somewhat obvious that all these illustrious reports are a bit of a ruse. (That's a nice way of saying that they're being somewhat reckless with the truth.)

The cliché, "kitchen sink economy," has been used to infer that since the stock market collapse of 2000, business and government have thrown everything but the kitchen sink at the economy in a resuscitation effort. That is a graphic description that couldn't be more accurate.

While we take an up-close-and-personal look at exactly what all has been thrown at reviving the great machine, keep in mind the side effects of induced inflation. The old people and the kids get hurt, those in the middle *think* that they are being helped, and what happens to the rich? You're on to that one — they get richer. Even economic wars experience casualties. But then we covered that. Now if *all* old people and kids got hurt in the game of inflation, it wouldn't be such a popular sport. But then we covered that too. *All* would suggest that Big Business, the politicians, and the college economics professors were joining us for the game — they're not. So let's take down the mirrors, blow away the smoke, and put a little light on the subject.

I mentioned the fact that General Motors, Ford, and Delphi, if not circling the drain, are certainly on that end of the tub. United, Delta, U.S. Air, and Northwest Airlines are in or just emerging from bankruptcy. Fuel of every description has gone berserk. Steel, copper, gold, platinum, lumber, aluminum, cement, beef, dairy products, education, and insurance are near record highs. I could go on and on, but I don't need to. I'm sure that at some time during the last year, all of you have been to the grocery, the gas station, the home improvement store, paid your home heating bill, and have attempted to balance your checkbook.

It is interesting that inflation, according to the consumer price index (CPI), for all of 2006, was reported as being 2.5% on a consumer level. We could have really been in trouble if inflation had been reported at say, 3%. Of course, the 2.5% growth in consumer prices doesn't include food or fuel. It does include housing, but that calculation was changed to Government Math in 1983. Rather than use the actual rise in the cost of current housing, after 1983, the government began measuring *rents* instead. You think I'm making this up, don't you? Huh-uh. That particular policy change was made due to the fact that voters don't like high inflation. If the government included food, fuel, and housing *fairly*, it would be evident that we *have* high inflation! That's a no brainer; give the people what they want. The government doesn't change the questions, they change the answers.

With core inflation for 2006 remaining at a low 2.5%, and early projections for 2007 being the same, those people who aren't dependent on fuel, food, or housing are in pretty darn good shape. Embalming fluid has that effect, doesn't it?

Do you ever wonder where these Government Math people come from? There is a special oral test that each of them have to pass for entry into the inner sanctum of the Advanced Government Math Headquarters. It goes like this: The examiner calls the brilliant mathematician prospect in and asks, "Reginald, what is two times two?" Reginald, or "Reggie," as the boys down at the country club call him, gets a puzzled look on his face and says, "I'm thinking...maybe four?" The interviewer then says, "Thank you, Reginald, don't call us, we'll call you."

This process is repeated until such a time that a special person who comprehends the complexities of Government Math arrives on the scene. The interviewer asks the special person, "Scamway, what is two times two?" Scamway looks slowly in all directions, and after being assured that they are alone, gets up and closes the office door. He comes back, leans across the desk, and whispers, "What do you want it be?" *Torture numbers, and they'll confess to anything.* — Gregg Easterbrook

Meanwhile, back at the ranch, G.M. and Ford are breaking out the life vests, and the market for iPods, Xboxes, and giant plasma screen TVs is nothing less than spectacular. If this is starting to appear to you as if the places where we make money are in trouble and the places where we spend that money for entertainment are on a roll, you'd be correct. "So how can that work?" You ask. About as well as it did for the Romans, and it's not called the *fall* of the Roman Empire for nothing. Remember, when I say that "all is *not* well," I am NEVER inferring that everyone involved in our system of commerce is sharing the pain equally. Here's a typical headline:

"Breaking news: As thousands of workers are asked to take a 95% pay reduction in light of Schmuckco Manufacturing's $1.2 billion loss last quarter, company President, Will B. Alright, was awarded $20 million as a bonus for agreeing to remain with the beleaguered company and assist in drafting an equitable workout plan."

In a news interview following the announcement, Mr. B. Alright stated, "It could have been worse; I could have only gotten $10 million." When asked what he thought of the plight of the workers, B. Alright responded, "I'd like to give them a hand, but I just can't reach that far. Ha-ha, just kidding." B. Alright continued by saying, "Schmuckco cannot be expected to take responsibility for our employees' failure to structure their personal lives at a level where losing their jobs and retirement would inconvenience them. After all, if you take away my money, my golden parachute pension plan, and my second home in Aspen, we're all in the same boat." "And there you have it, back to you in Washington, Dan."

"So," you say, "we know all about the position of the rich and famous, but you still haven't told us where all the jobs and money are coming from." We're going to have to go back and visit Earl and family to find that out.

The Scottish-born poet and novelist Andrew Lang said, "He uses statistics as a drunken man uses lampposts — for support rather than illumination." The American rendition of this quote is most surely, "Feed them bull and keep them in the dark." As for us, we need to change our diet and put a little light on the subject.

Money makes the world go round. Not literally, but it does make our commerce go around. It's a matter of providing the people more and more money and they'll spend it. That seems simple enough. All that is required is a perpetual supply of money and the means to pass it out. That brings us back to Earl and the year 2001.

Not that the economy had been all that whoopee for the period *preceding* the attack of 9/11/01. The United States had experienced a serious stock market collapse in 2000, referred to as the "Dot Com bubble bursting," and the country was still trying to trim up the haircut that American investors had taken on that one. Interestingly enough, a bunch of seemingly brilliant young upstarts, who either got out of the market early or were lucky enough to be between scams (I meant to say "investments"), became millionaires, which proves that "lucky" really is better than "good." It was after the attack on 9/11, though, that things really got dicey. The country fell into a state of paralysis and the money quit flowing.

The Fed (you remember those guys) had noticed that the 2000 stock market collapse was not a good thing. Fed governors pick up on such things about six months after the natives in New Guinea have the news. Once alerted to the fact that immediate action should have been taken six months prior, the

Fed sprang into action — at least as close to "springing" as quasi-government people can simulate.

The Fed's standard method of reestablishing a paralyzed society to its former "borrow and spend like a madman" is complex beyond the average American citizen's comprehension. That's why we have Fed governors to handle the heavy thinking. We will, however, overcome by reducing the process to an understandable format with Mikeronomics. I can do that, because I'm not your average citizen. I've had countless people tell me over the years that I'm not even *close* to being average.

Here's an example of the way it works. The Fed governors get together and the Fed Chairman opens by saying, "I have received word from a source in New Guinea that the fund rate is too high. How low do you think we should go?" The governors at this point rear back in their chairs and assume a posture of divine intelligence and philosophical thought for a period of time that rivals the mini Ice Age, after which they declare with grave seriousness, "We don't have a clue." The Chairman then turns to the secretary and says, "Monica, do you remember what we did the last time that this happened?" The secretary answers, "Uh...that was last month, sir, and reading directly from the minutes, all of you decided 'to just keep lowering the rate until those suckers start borrowing again.'" "Awesome idea," the Chairman announced. "And better news yet, we're going to get out of here early today."

Beginning in January of 2001, the Fed lowered the federal funds rate ten consecutive times, from 6% to 1.75%. You can see that this downward fishing expedition started a full eight months prior to the attack on 9/11. Even with the federal rate for funds sitting at 1.75%, a recovery did not appear imminent. By June 2003, the Fed had reduced the rate to 1%, the lowest since 1958.

Just prior to the economy being officially pronounced dead, a faint pulse was found. This period is often referred to as "the recovery that almost wasn't." I'd say that was putting it mildly. Mr. Bill Clinton was the President from January 20, 1993, to January 20, 2001. The Dot Com bubble had burst, the fishing expedition for reviving the economy had begun, and Mr. Clinton was luckily term limited and could later say, "I don't know what happened, it was alright when I left." Hasta luego.

The continual downward rate in interest did eventually breathe some life back into the economy, and no doubt the citizenry (and the illegal aliens) were once more spending money like drunken sailors. For those of you who take offense to the seemingly derogatory term "drunken sailor," I apologize. However, and admittedly on more than one occasion, I *was* one. And I can personally attest to the fact that the former suggestion that drunken sailors spend money with reckless abandon is a fairly accurate depiction.

Did I tell you why the stock market collapsed in 2000? To begin with, the whole thing was based on Charles Ponzi's business plan, but that's not the point that I want to make. In April 2000, the natives were already a little restless when the government released a surprisingly bad inflation report. Okay, *terrible* inflation report. All of the seasoned investors, which in 2000 meant that you had read the book *How to Become a Multi-Millionaire by Next Week in Dot Com Stocks*, did what anyone who realizes that they have just lost their life savings would do: PANIC. And panic they did, followed by the NASDAQ dropping 1,125 points and the DOW dropping 805 points in one week.

A lot of these seasoned investors that we spoke about had borrowed the money to get in on this unbelievable *gain*, which was now unbelievably *gone*. "Hey, isn't that what the investors did in the market crash of 1929?" Yes, they did, which proves that lightning really can strike in the same place twice.

It is truly important to understand the magnitude of difficulty that our government and Big Business had in reviving the economy after the 2000 crash. Consider this: in order to induce the public to borrow money, the Fed had reduced the funds rate to 1% in the year 2003! That move was a last resort, last-ditch effort. When the Fed got down to 1%, something had to catch fire soon. This is similar to the movie plot where the hero is freezing to death in a blizzard and has only one match — combustion is essential.

So what do low, low, interest rates accomplish? Not only is borrow and spend like a madman back in style, so is inflation. To compensate, Earl puts the night shift back on.

The sword of low interest-induced inflation is sharp on both sides. When the Fed rate is 1%, the folks that have interest-bearing investments are making zip point, *nada*. Of course, most of them were probably old people who didn't plan well.

The real point is that jump-starting the economy has become more and more difficult. The year 2003 was not all that long ago, and we darn near lost our last match. The government is still counting on you not to remember that. But we're going to let them down this time, aren't we?

During the same period that the Fed governors were doing their part by lowering the funds rate to 1%, the United States was engaged in a war over in Afghanistan, and eventually in Iraq. U.S. troops are still present in both areas at the time of this writing. Oh, no — I'm not going *there*. Whether the war is right or wrong is not going to be debated in these pages. It is the benefit of the war economy that I need to point out. I will say one thing, if we run out of gas in the good ol' U.S. of A., an economic war will come to a town near you quicker than a dog pound cat. I'm not necessarily talking about the gas that makes a car go; I'm talking about the gas that makes an economy go.

The effect that a war has on the economy is broad, and for our limited discussion, we can focus mainly on the fact that the government spends billions and billions of dollars on the effort. Thousands of civilians work at producing everything from bombs to buns, resulting in an expanded work force. Reserve soldiers, sailors, and airmen, who would normally be working, have been called away to serve. This creates vacancies in the jobs that they left behind, and the hiring of replacement personnel is required. The net effect is that thousands more people are on the payrolls of American companies and the Federal Government. "So when the new employment figures are given, does it discount those working purely due to the war effort?" You gotta be kidding! Jobs are hard enough to come by these days without doing any sorting; they count 'em where they find 'em.

Now, some of you mentioned the white-hot housing... "Whoa, whoa, hold on there. What happens when the war is over? Won't the replacement jobs go away and the military spending be diminished?" If I was taking a wild guess I would say, absolutely, you can bet your bottom dollar on it. That is, however, not necessarily the worst effect. The government spent billions and billions of dollars on the war effort, right? The government doesn't have any money. They have you and Earl. "Oh, jeez, we knew you were going to say that, and we just got the dang Visa card paid off."

Government debt and your credit card have more in common than you might think. When our government charges incessantly on their credit card (the National Debt), just like you, they also have to make a minimum monthly interest payment. The principal difference is, *you* have a *limit* on your card.

It isn't totally accurate to say that spending will go down after the war effort is ended. It *should* go down. However, *sufficient money to keep the show on the road has to come from somewhere.* Either the government has to continue to fund America's economy (on credit) or the private sector economy has to grow to a level that will produce sufficient *viable* jobs and taxes to offset the current deficits in government spending. What's that called? Sure, same answer, growth, growth, and more growth, and then additional growth. I'm thinking that we probably can't depend on G.M. and Ford to do that. Maybe the iPods, Xboxes, and plasma screen TVs will get the job done...oh, that's right; those things are made in China.

If all else fails (which it had), lower the interest rate, fan the flames of inflation, and heat up the domestic housing market. That ought to get the job done, at least long enough for the present administration to say, "It was alright when I left."

The housing market has been nothing but hot. Millions of Americans are making a better-than-average living building new homes in every corner of the country. Personal wealth in the form of reported home equity is climbing at a staggering rate. There are books, videos, and live seminars that explain the goriest details of how to make a small fortune in real estate.

Actually, it's easy to make a small fortune in real estate; go into it with a large fortune and limited knowledge and you will soon have a very small fortune.

"Flipping properties" is a household phrase today. This is America's future right here and now, and it's hotter than a two-dollar pistol. In some parts of Florida, houses are being bought in the morning and sold for a profit in the afternoon. Walt Disney created Fantasyland; America's housing industry stole his thunder. The Great American Dream is back on track like lightning in a jar. Let's see if we can keep from getting electrocuted.

If you aren't somewhat convinced by this point that exponential growth is never going to work long term, maybe I can muster up a more convincing argument using housing as an example. We all know something about housing. For instance, not having any is inconvenient. Camping can be fun for the weekend, but after about three days, a person can lose a little enthusiasm for eating burnt weiners in the rain and having your clothes and hair smell like what's being served for dinner at Tex's barbeque.

Housing, then, is no doubt a necessity. But is it necessary for each occupant to have 1,000 square feet of personal living space? Sure, it would be nice, but can we afford it and at the same time keep the general economy on track? What say we reduce this thing down to a common-sense format to get a more realistic view of the big picture?

Housing is as old as mankind. The necessity for housing has never changed. The earliest humans utilized housing as a means of climate control and to keep the critters out of their stuff. People thousands of years ago actually invented the mobile home (and were robbed of the credit for doing so, I might add). The principal difference back then was that the owner provided the necessary propulsion for the tepee or tent. "Well, Mom, I think we better move today. You round up the kids and I'll grab the house." Pretty darn convenient, and no taxes or mortgage payments at all.

Housing today provides the same basic elements that it provided the earliest man—climate control and keeping the critters out of our stuff, and boy do we have stuff. Somewhere between a tent and a 40,000 square foot mansion is the perfect domicile. I really don't like continually being the messenger of bad news, and I do keep promising some good news for some of you, but this just isn't the place to do it. Housing is a serious issue that is going to have HUGE future implications. You really do need to at least take a look at the downside. Not to worry, I'm not going to suggest that your future involve a portable house.

Housing is, of course, included in the sector of goods described as durable. My wife and I spent 15 happy years in a home that was constructed in 1926. Surely that qualifies as durable. We had made improvements and modifications over the years, but by and large, it was the same farmhouse that was originally built in '26. We weren't too cheap to buy a new house; it's that we didn't NEED a new house. We were warm and dry and successfully fended off the critters.

We have established that houses meet the criteria for durable goods, with the exception of the disposable homes that were discussed in an earlier chapter. That being said, and hazarding a guess that no one wants to purposely corner the market on vacant homes, the housing market needs constant population growth to survive. Simply put, homes need homeowners.

Fortunately for us, the average lifespan for Americans keeps increasing. If folks had an earlier demise, their homes would become available for the live ones much sooner, and fewer new homes would be needed. Thankfully, Dad and Mom, Grandpa and Grandma, and Great-Grandma and Great-Grandpa are all still using their homes simultaneously and won't let the kids move in with them, which, in turn, increases demand for new housing.

We need continual increases in prospective new homeowners in order to keep all the workers who build homes *working*. This goes for all the people who make the things that we build homes with, such as windows, doors, carpet, drywall, roofing, cement, lumber, and towel bars. So here is the question: what happens when everyone who wants a home has one?

Let's just kid ourselves a little and say that that will never happen. Ha-ha. To help us believe that demand will never decrease, let's also say that we will become much more tolerant to immigration and allow 2 million people to come to the United States every year. Now, here's the new question: what happens when everyone who can *afford* a new home has one? Yep, same answer to both questions: OH, MY GOD!

Let's go even further out on our precarious limb and say the economy is going to get sooooo good, and that immigration is going to be increased by sooooo much, that we will never reach a point that housing demand will decline. That will, in turn, keep all the people who build homes, and all the people who make things to build homes with, working forever. Would everyone who believes even one teensy weensy bit of that last statement hold up your hands? For those two people who have their hands up, you have just passed through Fantasyland and gone into the Twilight Zone. What goes up, must come down.

"So now, Mr. I Have Some Bad News, you never answered our question of where are all of the home buyers are coming from?" They were here all the time. They just couldn't afford a house. "So the economy is improving at that, huh?" No, but the mortgage rates certainly are. We have determined that inflation has existed ever since the government needed a way to get more money, which is forever. Wages had inflated along with everything else, but not nearly as fast as home prices. Mortgage interest had also increased over the years, and the combination was putting the squeeze play on housing in the form of un-affordability.

The Fed realized that simply lowering the price of housing would temporarily get them out of a bind. Acting on this new stroke of brilliance, the Fed asked America's builders to consider lowering their profits and therefore reducing the price of housing. The builders discussed the possibility for 10 seconds and said, "Does the mental institution know that you people are out?"

The Fed took that as a no. Going back to the drawing board, a new plan was hatched. As we saw previously, the Fed rode the time machine back to 1958 and made money sooooo cheap that people who really couldn't afford a house could buy one anyway. And, the people who already had a home could buy a bigger improved model. A lot bigger.

Remember, some of these Fed governors only needed one more clean shirt until retirement, so long-term planning had, let's say, lost some of its appeal. I know there are some people out there saying that the federal funds rate does not control long-term mortgage interest and primarily affects only short-term rates. And, that T-bills and bond rates correlate more closely to the rates charged for long-term debt.

That is fundamentally true, but the correlation between short-term and long-term interest rates is nonetheless closely associated, and for our discussion, we aren't going into a lengthy dissertation about every factor that affects rates. I do point out that it was not by coincidence that 30-year fixed mortgage rates dropped to a 45-year record low of 4.75% in June 2003, right along with the Federal Funds rate of 1% at the same time.

The result of the Fed tweaking the system provided lower mortgage rates and allowed the opportunity for thousands of additional Americans to purchase new housing. But the sword was sharp on both sides, and those who had previously counted on interest income became casualties of the Fed's financial policy.

To sweeten the pot, a couple of other characters named Fannie Mae and Freddie Mac (corporations who purchase mortgage loans in the secondary market) provided the necessary backing to keep the show on the road.

Further assistance was given to those who REALLY couldn't afford a home by offering 3- and 5-year adjustable rate loans, and interest-only mortgages. Heck, the way this thing is going, three years from now the homes would be worth 50% more and the person borrowing the money would surely be making higher wages to support the higher payments. A common phrase for this type of creative financing was borrowed from the game of craps, and is stated as "betting on the come." And all this time I thought gambling was illegal.

The time machine to 1958 had hit warp speed. The re-finance business for existing mortgages went absolutely berserko. Thousands of additional people were employed in the businesses of appraisal, mortgage loans, home inspection, real estate, title companies, and an endless list of others. All we need is more people and more money to keep this puppy running like a greyhound.

Where was it that the people got all this money to buy new houses? Right, they borrowed it; for a long, long time. Okay, now that everyone in America can get into a home by taking advantage of zero down and interest only loans, I want to talk about a new problem of which I will wager you have never read a word. I'm not referring to the fact that the 3- and 5-year adjustable rate mortgages will soon ratchet upward and that the payments will have gone up far faster than wages, or that the interest-only mortgages will be even worse. I'm not even referring to the fact that taxes, utilities, and insurance will continue to outpace income.

It's that all of these people who now have HUGE house payments have promised to make those payments for 30 years or more. Many *existing* homeowners have cumulatively taken out an estimated $2 TRILLION in home equity loans, on *top* of their mortgages!

The MAJORITY of the average homeowners' income will service the *single* purpose of paying for, and maintaining, shelter. "And your point is?" And my point is, if an inordinate amount of a family's income is going purely to service home debt, where is money NOT going? Savings comes to mind.

On the surface, this may not seem like a big problem, but it is. Building a home has the most benefit to our economy during construction. This offers work to countless people such as the developers, builders, real estate agents, title companies, appraisers, engineers, and building suppliers. However, after the home is complete, the majority of the financial benefit to society ceases to exist. All of the aforementioned occupations have to go find another new homeowner if they want to collect another paycheck next Friday.

Once the home is complete, most of the homeowner's money is being devoted to interest, and only benefits the lender.

Therefore, having an inordinate portion of the general publics' earnings committed long term to any single purpose has the effect of robbing money from other sectors within that same economy. The cumulative effect of funneling the majority of a family's earnings into shelter alone creates the very real possibility of bankrupting entire sectors of nonessential commerce.

This of course would not be the case if incomes could constantly grow, but even Earl has some limitations, particularly in this current era of world trade. Government reports for the third quarter of 2005 stated that for the first time since 1932, savings had gone negative in the United States. The average person is spending more annually than they are making. This is a startling statistic, and yet gets little press. Why? It's bad news for business.

A writer for the *Wall Street Journal* declared that he thought perhaps in 2006 Americans would save more money. I can see that. With all the bargains that we are receiving on fuel, groceries, utilities, housing, and transportation, saving more in future years should prove a cinch. Well..., maybe not. Year end figures for 2006 disclosed that negative savings dropped even further into the red ink. I think the *Journal* author has potential for passing the Government Math test.

The fact that personal savings have dipped below zero for two consecutive years is not a coincidence or a temporary situation. Hidden costs of inflation are pushing everyday living expenses beyond average current incomes. Our lifestyles will have to change; like the weary boxer, growth will fail to answer the bell in the very near future.

We're going to have to come back to real estate in a later chapter when we discuss what not to do. But before we leave this subject, hold your nose and we'll swallow one more dose of bad news. The great real estate boom that has allowed our domestic economy to stagger back onto its feet is ill founded for more reasons than I have pages to write on. For those of you who didn't enter the Twilight Zone earlier on this subject, it won't surprise you to learn that there is a predictable end, and it isn't pretty.

There is an enormous difference between commercial/industrial, and residential real estate in regard to how each serves the public good. Residential real estate serves only to provide shelter to the individual members of our society, and as we saw, it has the greatest benefit to public good (in regard to commerce) during construction.

Commercial/industrial real estate, on the other hand, represents the very heart of the commerce that provides the incomes used to pay the new homeowners mortgages. Growth in commercial/industrial real estate, then, is essential to supporting the income required for growth in the residential real estate sector. (The picky mortgage people insist that having a job helps a person qualify for the loan.) The current boom that we are experiencing, and the record-beating inflation in real estate, are by and large confined to the residential sector. Even the Government Math gurus may not be able to spin that information into a positive. What am I thinking? Of course they can.

As building costs continue to escalate, which they must, and as interest rates continue to climb, which they will, and as qualified buyers begin to diminish, which has already begun — what happens? Those people who entered the real estate market utterly dependent on continual increases in their home values and personal wages will realize that they have taken a very costly gamble. The Federal Government's purposeful introduction of inflation by slashing interest rates to 1958 lows, combined with relaxing lending standards, will be the undoing of thousands of homeowners who are up to their eyeballs in housing debt.

Here's the question again: "If 500 workers are building an unsold condo project, what do they do after they finish?" Go fishing. You can *eat* those things, you know.

CHAPTER 8

TIME AND MATERIALS

IF YOU AREN'T CONVINCED BY NOW that we're cruisin' for a bruisin', and if you still have a book that is readable after gnawing on the cover and dashing it to the floor in fits of frustration, keep reading. As they say on the TV offer: "WAIT! There's more."

The phrase "time and materials" is used to describe one means by which charges are made for a given project. For instance, an electrician who wires a building on a time-and-materials contract will, on completion, determine the time that was spent on the job along with the materials that were consumed and bill accordingly. I don't recommend this approach for having your house wired, due to the very real possibility of the electrician becoming so familiar around your home that your kids begin calling him "Uncle Sparky." But the phrase does have a startling correlation to our ongoing economy.

We'll take a peek at the "materials" part of the "time-and-materials" equation first. To make the great engine that propels our economy run, we need to feed it fuel — lots and lots of fuel. Unlike the engine in your car, the big engine that drives our economy is a multi-fuel model and burns every naturally occurring material on planet earth — lumber, cement, copper, steel, gold, water, air, and so on. It also burns renewable materials such as wheat, oats, corn, beef, pork, chickens, and hot dogs.

The more folks that inhabit our planet, the more growth, growth, growth that we require, and consequently, the more fuel the old girl burns. For those of you who are politically sensitive, the term "old girl" is used affectionately in this case. For those of you who are still upset, the rest of this book is going to become far too graphic for your sensibilities. Actually, maybe not; by the time we get to the end, you may be using language that would hurt *my* sensibilities.

The big engine of our economy runs like a watch, so long as whoever is in charge of fueling doesn't let her run out of gas. Just keep feeding that lumber into the firebox and adding oil, and we'll all be fine. You're already bracing yourself for the new bad news, aren't you? Pull that seat belt extra tight, because this bump is going to send us airborne. I mentioned "naturally occurring" resources a moment ago, meaning that whatever came with this big old spaceship that we call "earth" is all that we have in stock. Shipments from the moon have been delayed due to technical difficulties.

So what happens when you use up anything that can't be replenished? Permanent backorder. Running empty on natural resources will be a particularly annoying event. Well, annoying for anyone who is under the age of 80. I bet that was a relief for a bunch of our fearless leaders in Washington.

There have been ongoing debates since the beginning of modern time regarding the sustainability of natural resources on our little planet. Science is a lot like statistics, it is...what do we say here?...somewhat flexible. There are enough scientific (and *not* so scientific) theories and studies in print dealing with sustainability to fill the remainder of your life with reading material, and what would you gain? Eye strain and a more confused state than when you began. So to save time and your eyes, I'll reduce the entire problem to Mikemathics. — *It requires a very unusual mind to undertake the analysis of the obvious.* — Alfred North Whitehead

Alfred North Whitehead was an English born philosopher and mathematician who apparently possessed a little more common sense than most. Mr. Whitehead saw some of our most complex problems as being obvious. He also saw that the highly practiced ostrich approach was having a less than desirable outcome in dealing with those problems.

I know that you have heard at least a few people say similar things to this: "There is oil enough in Texas alone to last the world another thousand years, and they could produce gas for 25 cents per gallon if they wanted to. But nooooo, them dang big ol' oil companies are plottin' against us and spent $8 billon to build the Alaska Pipeline, just so they could git out of payin' Uncle Billy Bob the royalties on his oil well." If any of these people who say this are your neighbors, I'd keep a close eye on them if I were you. If they happen to be relatives, there isn't much you can do about that except refuse to let your kids stay overnight at their place.

People who believe stories like the one I just mentioned are normally somewhat mathematically challenged. Just imagine a conversation between oil company executives that would go like this: "Bobby Roy, should we just drive out to old Harold Eugene's ranch and pump some of that cheap Texas crude, or take one of them big ol' boats halfway around the world and buy some from them nice A-rab fellers?" "Well, cousin Earl John, I'm thinking that buying that oil from them nice A-rab fellers would cost about twice as much, and we wouldn't make near the profit, so why don't we do just that, us being good ol' boys and trying to do our part for world commerce?" If you believe that, I've got a bridge for sale.

The truth is that we can't produce enough oil in America to fuel that engine that we talked about a moment ago. With every year that passes the problem gets worse, yet the fact that oil is a finite resource that would eventually be depleted has been known for years. In 1956 the American geophysicist, Dr. Marion King Hubbert, wrote an important paper that has become known as "Hubbert's Curve." Mr. Hubbert predicted that U.S. oil production would peak in 1970, and that *peak* world production would be reached by the year 1995. He was, of course, branded for the kook that he obviously was, and eventually was proven quite wrong. While he was dead-on regarding U.S. oil production (U.S. production peaked in 1970), peak world oil production is thought by many industry experts to have occurred in 2005! While Mr. Hubbert could not have possibly predicted the exact date of peak oil production in the world, being off by only ten years on his predictions of 44 years into the future ain't bad.

Oil is one of those "naturally occurring" resources that I talked about. The problem with having an infinite appetite for anything that is finite in nature is obvious: you flat run out. Oil is at the top of the list for resources that fall into that category. Mr. Hubbert also distinguished between *physical* oil reserves and the *recoverable* oil on earth.

To better understand what *recoverable* meant to Dr. Hubbert, this is what he said: "There is a different and more fundamental cost that is independent of the monetary price. That is the energy cost of exploration and production. So long as oil is used as a source of energy, when the energy cost of recovering a barrel of oil becomes greater than the energy content of the oil, production will cease no matter what the monetary price may be."

There are few arguments against the fact that we will deplete world oil at some point — as to when, the jury is still out. But the longer they are out, the smarter Marion King Hubbert is becoming. For any of you who have bought any gas or home-heating fuel in the last few years, the price would indicate that Dr. Hubbert has predicted something far more correct than we would like to believe. And speaking of beliefs, this would be a good time to consider whether you have more belief in your neighbor who is related to Uncle Billy Bob or the now-proven predictions of Dr. Hubbert.

What goes for oil also goes for iron ore, copper, fresh water, and all the rest of the finite resources. What we have is all that we will ever have. So then, is growth, growth, growth and more growth a problem for non-renewable resources? Alfred North Whitehead would say, "Obviously." But then, we know the obvious answer won't advance growth, so let's work up a math problem to determine the politically correct answer.

Question: If Mary has 100 gallons of gasoline which represents all of the gas on earth, and wants to divide the gasoline equally with her 50 classmates, how many gallons of gas would each classmate get?

Mikemathics answer: None. Mary determined that dividing the gasoline would result in a riot and create racial tensions as to who received the most gas based on color, creed, and country of origin. Rather than generate an unnecessary squabble, Mary decided that for the good of her classmates, she would use all of the gasoline herself on a road trip to Cancun. Mary is a graduate student at Harvard Law School with aspirations of becoming a U.S. Senator.

Government Math Answer: 500 gallons each. The theory for this answer was provided by Government Mathematicians and PhDs in economics who will all be retiring in four and a half years: Congress will mandate that Mary put the gasoline in storage tanks for five years prior to distribution. Government calculated growth and inflation predictions for the five-year storage period indicate that the very properties of growth and inflation will expand the gasoline supply to 5,000 gallons, giving Mary's classmates 500 gallons each.

As long as we have Government and Big Business, we'll never be at a loss for humorous material. But we need to get back to the business of harvesting natural resources. One of the answers for relieving the pressure of supplying natural resources on a continually expanding basis has been to get a bigger truck. Not exactly like our previous story, but then, not far off. The accepted method for increasing production to meet demand for such minerals as coal, iron ore, gold, and copper is to continually increase the size of the equipment used to harvest and transport the subject resources.

Underground coal mines for instance, with the use of modern "long-wall" mining techniques, can mine more coal in a 10-hour shift than the old time coal miners could mine in a year! The advent of bodacious machinery has made it possible to move entire mountains in only a few years. Iron ore from Minnesota is dug by enormous power shovels and shipped to China (yep, China) on super freighters that grow in size as the demand for iron ore grows. Problem solved, huh? Not so much as you could notice. You see, the supply doesn't change. We still have just exactly the same amount that came with our planet, less, of course, the amount that we use every day.

Bigger machinery *will* certainly answer the long-anticipated question a whole lot sooner of what will occur when we run out of any given resource. I figure that this is the type of problem that more or less solves itself. What do you do when you are 100 miles from a gas station, there are no cars on the road, you run out of a critical resource (gas), and it is 50 below zero? You see, the problem solves itself. You freeze to death and you don't need anymore fuel.

The hard fact is that we are going to run out of resources far sooner than one may like to believe. Unless, of course, you are a person that has great faith in "They." When I discuss these subjects with the general public, I always get a few who say, "I'm not worried, *they'll* come up with something." A word of caution here: I personally know "They," and I would not put a great deal of confidence in "They" coming to the rescue.

The other common belief is that "They" have *already* come up with something and are just holding back until the time and the price are right. I'm not sure how old that "They" are going to be when the time and price get right, but I'm betting that if "They" don't trot out the idea real soon, dying with the secret is a very real possibility.

Many people tend to believe what they want to, and certainly without letting common sense get in their way. More often than not, humans believe what is most beneficial to their own personal situation and that which requires the least amount of effort. Let me put that in a different context, people choose diets that promise the maximum weight loss, while eating anything they like, and which doesn't include exercising. It doesn't work, but it fulfils the human need to put the world on notice that they haven't totally overlooked the obvious problem, but are instead simply trying to find the least painful way to deal with it. Most times, quick and easy just doesn't get it done.

The belief that "They" will come up with a new food source, fuel source, water source, building material source, etc., is not based on science or math, and certainly not on common reason; it is a concept that alleviates perceived personal pain. The thought of losing social status, power, and wealth for many people is a concept worse than the thought of death. If a person were to admit that we as a group are heading down the wrong path, lifestyle changes would have to be made. Personal jets, mansions, yachts, Hummers, and similar symbols of wealth would have to be given up for the good of those who will come after us, and even a few of those who are currently with us. So what do you think the chances are of getting the rich and famous to lay off flying their personal jets to an impromtu cocktail party? You are familiar with the term "fat chance," are you not?

Nope, it just isn't going to happen, as in, not an option. Most who live in vast excess (like our federal politicians) believe deep down that he or she will be the survivors of the game, and that is what it is really about. The very rich who in many ways control the world believe that in the end, they can salvage their way of life. I'm thinking they are wrong.

I can imagine that you may be questioning my belief that we are on the fast track for running out of resources. Surely, you think, we wouldn't just now be hearing it from ol' Mike, right? Not necessarily. Remember the point where we talked about the politician who had to tell all the good people that cornmeal mush was going to be a mainstay in their new diet? Huh-uh, way too much pain in that plan.

It often helps to get things down to a scale that fits into our personal lives in order to get a better handle on the big picture. We'll use oil as an example to examine the commonsense approach to considering the possibility for exhaustion of a finite resource. Oil lies in pools deep under the earth's surface. The large pools are called "giants" and the massive pools are "super giants." Most of the oil recovered on earth has come from these large pools. However, of the 48 major oil producing countries in the world, 33 are currently in decline from their peak production.

For our example, imagine having a large pond in your backyard that represents your own personal giant (we wish).Every day you pump out a little oil without putting any back. In the beginning, it certainly could seem that your oil would last forever. But as the years go by, your lifestyle includes using larger amounts of the oil every day (you bought a motor home). At some point, it would become obvious that you were depleting the pool and that an end is evident. The total supply of oil on the planet is absolutely no different. Everyone in the world is consuming the same finite supply, and when it's gone, it's gone — just that simple.

For years, the United States was the standout forerunner in the concerted effort to pump the oil pools dry, and we remain so today on a per capita basis. The United States represents slightly over 4% of the world population, yet uses approximately 25% of the global energy. As a country, the United States could have easily wiped out all of the natural resources single-handedly, and in good time. Today with the help of China, India, and a host of other emerging nations, we should be able to make even shorter work of the process.

Natural resources have been at the heart of our growth and development since the beginning of time. The human population multiplies and the resources decline. If you keep adding fish to the same bowl in order to achieve growth, you're eventually going to run long on fish and short on water, and the fish aren't going to like it. If adding people to the planet is our grand plan, "They" had better come up with a way to accomplish it without using finite natural resources, or the people aren't going to like the end result any better than the fish.

At the beginning of the second millennium (AD 1000), the world population was 400 million. In 1750, or 750 years later, that number doubled to 800 million. Then in the next hundred years, in 1850, there were a *billion* more, and by 1950, another billion. After which, *it took just 50 years to double to 6 billion*. In another 50 years, the world population is expected to be 9 billion. So how much is a billion? In this year 2007, a billion *seconds* ago was 1975!

In the above example, the latter number of 9 billion people projected to live on earth in another 50 years, would indicate that the future annual population growth is going to slow as compared to the previous 50 years. That's good, right? Apparently not in Japan. After WWII, the Japanese government decided "If you can't beat 'em, join 'em," and jumped square in the middle of capitalism.

What does it take to make Japanese capitalism work? More and more consumers, just like the good ol' U.S.of A. Leave it to the Japanese women to throw a wrench in the gears. Can you imagine the women in Japan having second thoughts about staying home and having babies? Who would have ever thought that they would want equal rights? They not only wanted equal rights, but their own careers. The nerve! Japan's birthrate fell to a record low of 1.29 children per couple in 2003.

As improved career opportunities gave Japanese women options other than marriage, many chose careers. Some would say that choosing a career over marriage wasn't a difficult decision, but I, being a happily married man, don't say anything. Oh, another item that you may find hard to believe is that many Japanese families put off having children, due to the difficulties of finding affordable child care and weak support for working mothers from companies and communities. And here you thought the United States had the corner on that market.

So what did the government of one town do about this situation? In the northern Japanese town of Yamatsuri, the local government will pay the equivalent of $9,600 to mothers who will agree to have a third child. The mother receives half when the baby is born, then $480 per year for the next ten years. This example is living proof of the importance for growth in a society that is based on ever-greater consumption and the need to pass the debt baton to the next generation. The more, the merrier.

Thankfully, in America we don't embrace such silly policies. Or do we? I probably should have included this tidbit of information in Chapter 7, Smoke and Mirrors. For those of you who pay taxes, and for those of you who made the decision not to pay taxes and will be getting out of jail soon, I'm sure you have noticed that reduced taxes favor those who have the highest number of dependents. ("Dependents" in this case should be considered to be children and not government officials.) In a free country such as the United States, a person could mistakenly assume that having children is a choice, and that the person making that choice has also chosen to support and educate those children. That assumption would be incorrect.

Those who don't have *any* children pay considerably more taxes than the people who do. The more children, the more tax breaks. This is the Government's way of "rewarding" the people without children, for not creating an overcrowding problem at the school. This same logic is applied to welfare. The more children a couple has, the less likely they are to have income sufficient to pay the cost of supporting those children, and the more likely they are to require public assistance.

So if those who have a few kids pay *fewer* taxes, and those who have lots of kids don't pay *any* taxes, who does that leave to pay taxes? Look at it this way: the people who physically have the kids in their possession are stressed out enough without having to come up with all the money necessary to support them. So you see, you just thought that the Federal Government didn't pay for having children. This is commonly called, "the indirect approach." Keep those little shoppers coming.

The second part of our time and materials subject is "time." The statement, "Time is of the essence," is contained in many legal contracts. It means simply that there are elements of the contract that are time sensitive. Elements that, if not attended to within a specified time, will jeopardize the contract. Life is a lot like that contract: there are certain aspects that are very time sensitive — breathing, for instance. Live it or lose it, there are no "do-overs."

I believe that "time" is the most misunderstood element in our lives. If we truly had the ability to comprehend time, we would live very differently. But not unlike forgetting the important fact that the economy was in the tank only a few years ago, we also forget to include time as an element in decision making. *You may delay, but time will not.* – Benjamin Franklin

Time, in fact, is the stuff that life is made of. In my opinion, this is the most important point in this book, and also the most difficult to comprehend. It certainly is for me. If a person can comprehend time as it relates to every aspect of their lives, the rest is easy. That sounds kind of wacky, doesn't it? The sort of thing that you might find on the note inside a fortune cookie. I can tell fortunes. No, *really* I can. So you don't believe me, huh? Here's one: "He who believes that 'They' will arrive with the answer has no idea what the question is."

To understand time is as close as I believe that one can come to knowing the storied "secret to the universe." A failure to understand the relationship that time has on our long-term, as well as daily, decision making, will cause your life to stop at an inconvenient and unplanned location. *If you find that you're on the wrong train, get off at the next stop. It makes getting back home a much shorter trip.* — Mike Folkerth

If I were asked what I thought man's most important intangible possession was, I would answer, without hesitation, "happiness." If I were asked what the most important single aspect of knowledge one should acquire to obtain happiness was, I would say, "the understanding of time."

Few would argue that happiness is the pinnacle of a life well lived; *without* happiness, what is there? *With* happiness, what more can be achieved? I promise, it really *is* that simple.

Comprehending the very real possibility that we may well run out of time (like, be dead) before we get happy is not so simple. The thought of getting dead prior to getting happy sort of knocks the bloom off the whole process, doesn't it?

The real problem is that most of us believe that we will live forever, and sometime during forever, our circumstances will magically change for the best and we'll be happy. I'm thinking that many people are counting on "They" coming along and making everything all better. Unfortunately, "They" are a big fan of Halloween, and more often than not, show up in the Grim Reaper costume just prior to the point that we were going to be happy.

We get sidetracked on little 30-year excursions that take up a whole lot of our happy time. If I were limited to one single subject of which I could write and teach, it would be "Time." So again, it is the absolute understanding of time as it applies to our lives that would go far in people acquiring that most cherished possession — happiness.

I bet some of you thought I was going to say that our most cherished possession for acquiring happiness was a new car. It's not even in the top one thousand. But that is a good subject to demonstrate our total disconnect with time. When you buy that brand new, high-end, state-of-the-art car, the new smell wears off in about five weeks, the car payment wears off in about five years, and the value wears off in about five minutes. Good deal, huh? Dumb, dumb, dumb.

Buying new cars is a loser's sport, like a hustler with a corner shell game. Do you want to lose your hard-earned money buying a car that will rob you of your fun time? Everyone is emphatically shaking their heads NOOOO except for the car dealers in the crowd. So why do we do it over and over? We think that the happy euphoric feeling that one has when they drive home a new car will last indefinitely. We are willing to trade five years of payments, high-priced insurance and plates, and staggering losses to be happy. Of course, it isn't true, but our near-total disconnect with time allows us to believe differently.

The loss on a new car pales in comparison to believing "The Biggest Lie Ever Believed." The car illusion lasts for 60 months of car payments and the work-now-and-be-happy-later illusion lasts one day longer than you will. I shouldn't say longer than *you* will, because you aren't going to go that route, are you? Come on — I know a shortcut that will get us there way ahead of the crowd.

We will visit the important subject of time frequently as we go forward. Before we leave this chapter, though, I want to help you understand time on a very broad scale that will hopefully assist you to see the impossibility of continuing our present course of exponential consumption.

Humans have inhabited the earth for more than 30,000 years. *Recorded* history began some 4,000 years ago. Yet just a little more than a hundred years *prior* to today, or the single lifetime of some living humans, man had little ability to extract natural resources in quantity. Flight was not possible, horses were still very much in use, and electricity was relatively new. It is paramount to comprehend this time-line in order to clearly understand what is sustainable, or even remotely mathematically *possible*, and what is not.

When we talk about the ups and downs of our historical economy, we are normally talking about the last 55 years, or that economy which began shortly after WWII, which was up and running by 1950. This is the time frame that seems the most difficult to get our arms around. BUT, once you totally comprehend the short time frame that our present economy has existed, it will become an invaluable tool to predicting the future with some certainty.

Prior to WWI (August 1914 to November 1918), humans had little ability to create massive commerce. The industrial revolution that had begun to fuel the modern economy was in its infancy. After the end of WWI, the cessation of the war-induced commerce caused the United States and Canadian economies to fall into a deep, but short, recession that within two years gave way to the "roaring twenties." By 1922, it appeared that America was on the path of phenomenal growth and prosperity. This perceived prosperity lasted less than eight years and, instead of affluence, gave way to the beginning of the Great Depression in 1929. The depression economy lingered for 12 long years. This period became known as the "dirty thirties," and was only interrupted by America's entry into WWII (December 7, 1941 to September 2, 1945). It was not until after WWII that the modern economy, which we most often refer to, truly began. Pretty short and sweet, isn't it?

So it is evident that during the short lifetime of the first crop of baby-boomer kids, the vast majority of our *current* American commerce has materialized. Not over thousands, nor hundreds, nor even one hundred years, but, instead, 60 short years. That should help you to better consider how much longer we can possibly operate under "The Biggest Lie Ever Believed."

Consider that in just 80 years — from 1950 to 2030, (with all things remaining constant) — we will have extracted more than 75% of all known oil reserves in the world. We will also have reduced many other natural resources to near extinction. In the lifetimes of those humans who will spend 2% of the *recorded* man's time on earth, we will use the *majority* of the known natural resources on this planet.

I'm not saying that we will be *out* of resources in the next few years; we won't. What I am saying is that if China, India,

Mexico, Korea, Japan, Russia, etc., etc., continue to industrialize at or above their current levels, there soon won't be enough to go around for everyone in the world. Who at that point gets to determine the divvying up process?

The United States represents slightly more than 4% of the world population. We also *import* as much as 75% of our annual oil requirements, oil that belongs to another nation. Just a reminder.

Reducing the subject of depletion to Mikeronomics, what happens when there is an orange crop failure in Florida? We look at the price of orange juice and suddenly acquire a new appreciation for water. There *is* orange juice available, but it requires filling out loan papers to buy a gallon. The difference between oranges and natural resources is that we'll have another crop of oranges coming on next year. But what the world has coming on is another crop of consumers.

The illustrations above demonstrate that the process of extracting resources for the sole purpose of spurring growth will be short lived. We need to adapt to our finite world, or in the not-so-distant future, the real possibility exists that the manager at the supermarket will have to say, "I'm sorry folks, we are out of groceries. I hope that doesn't inconvenience anyone."

CHAPTER 9

SOCIAL INSECURITY AND MAYBECARE

IF YOU STILL AREN'T CONVINCED that growth is not the answer to our continued success and happiness as a species, you are most likely employed in the upper echelons of Government or Big Business, and have read this far just to see if I had intentions of messing up your deal. Thank you very much — I'd love to!

Once we take the time to stop and take a long and concerted look at some of the wacky fixes that have been applied to our economic woes, considering mandatory psychiatric exams for our policy makers seems a justifiable requirement. Politicians as a whole just plainly don't have any better ideas — at least none which if practiced, would keep them in office. I *do* believe that if the point came that the Federal Government had express knowledge that our economy was going to collapse in 12 months, they would wait eleven and a half months to tell us. No sense ending the party before it is absolutely necessary.

The behavioral influence of power, wealth, and greed is unfathomable to those who have either chosen not to partake in such activities, or perhaps, never had the opportunity. We have also become so entrenched in our growth-oriented economy that we literally have both hands and both feet stuck in the tar baby (for those of you who haven't read the tar baby story, it is a vivid example, told by Uncle Remus, of having both hands and feet caught in a trap). Any attempt to adopt a more sustainable economic model would require an enormous cultural change. The very suggestion of such a change would meet strong resistance, particularly among those who benefit most from our current illusion.

In many ways, we all know that our system is nearing the predictable end of the pyramid scheme that it is built on. We may not care to admit it, but we do recognize the symptoms. Social Security and Medicare may be more appropriately called Social Insecurity and Maybecare.

The foundations for Social Security and Medicare were built on the same swamp as our economy. I need to ask you a few questions to determine where you personally stand on a couple of topics. Okay, everyone who believes that Social Security is going to be around for your kids to enjoy, please hold up your hands. HELLO, I said every...wait, there is a gentleman in the back with his hand up. So, sir, do you actually believe that Social Security is in good health? Seriously? You really do? I'm sorry, Mr. Bush, I don't think we can allow you to weigh in on that question. So, that is 285 million voting No and one Yes vote. Just a moment, we do have two phone-in votes. Yes, Mr. Clinton and Mr. Carter, we'll be sure and tell them that it was alright when you left.

Here's the second question. How many of you believe that medical insurance is affordable? Uh, huh, same results, with two people in favor. Mr. Bush, I'm afraid we're going to have to ask you and Mr. Trump to abstain from these votes.

This is the final question. Would everyone who believes that Medicare and Medicaid can, under any circumstances, be funded over the next 20 years, please hold up your hand? Counting the yes votes, there does seem to be several people who believe that both Medicare and Medicaid are in good financial shape. Let me rephrase the question. Would everyone, besides the drug companies and the American Medical Association representatives, who believes that Medicare and Medicaid can be successfully funded over the next 20 years, please raise your hand? Just as I expected; no one else believes that will happen.

We all know that these programs will reach a mathematical impasse. Government economists have even set the date for when it will happen. The Medicare fund will be exhausted in 2019 and Social Security in 2041. Say what? "You mean we *know* when these programs will turn turtle and aren't doing

anything about it?" Yeah, I'd say that was an accurate statement. "Holymoly, that's terrible." "Terrible" is one of the kindest
things that can be said about the situation. "Horrific" is a word
that seems more appropriate. "So why don't they do something
about it?" you ask. Now we're getting somewhere. Shall we analyze that last question? Why don't "THEY" do something about
it? I warned you about counting on "They."

But to answer the question, "They" don't do anything about it
because "They" *can't* do anything about it. Sure, the Federal Government could assign a few Government Math experts to predict
that growth would solve the problem, but even the Government
Math guys have run out of imagination on that subject.

What's interesting about Social Security is that even politicians
have been telling us for years that it won't work! This is called
the "I-told-you-so" approach, for trying to keep the messengers
respective party in office after both of the programs crash.

President Bush, who wants to privatize Social Security accounts, may well have known that his plan would never find a
home. What a stroke of genius. Identify an impossible problem,
trot out a solution that will be shouted down, and then be able
to say, "What more could I have done? I told you we were going
to run out of money under the current program guidelines."

Social Security tax rate has been raised from the original 1935
rate of 2% to the 2006 rate of 12.4%, plus 2.9% for Medicare,
or 15.3% total. Social Security tax is currently paid on annual
earned incomes of up to $94,200, while Medicare tax has no
upper income limit cutoff.

Over the years, the minimum age for collecting *full* Social
Security benefits and Medicare has been raised in varying de-
grees, depending on the taxpayer's date of birth. For those born
in, or prior to 1937, it remains at the original age of 65. The
age for full benefits then adjusts upward in several increments
according to date of birth, to a current high of 67 for those born
after 1959. As you can see, the rules are subject to change.

I should make the point that Social Security won't suddenly
be out of money in 2041; there just won't be enough income to
match the outgo. Current projections indicate that either taxes

will have to be increased or benefits cut, or both, for Social Security to remain solvent after 2041. You may remember that Charles Ponzi had the same problem.

What happened to Social Security? How many of you have heard that the government has been robbing the money out of the Social Security fund? Just as I suspected, nearly everyone has heard that. How many of you believe that statement to be true? Yep, nearly everyone again; but it's not true.

Although it is a common belief that the fund was robbed, the government *by law* must borrow the funds and repay the loan plus interest. As money is needed to pay Social Security benefits, the Federal Government repays the fund. If this were not a requirement, inflation would long ago have reduced the Social Security reserves to pennies on the dollar. Thus far, government has funded Social Security as required.

The idea is that the interest on the borrowed Social Security funds (which is added to the National Debt), accompanied by continual growth, will more than provide for payment. Sure, it will.

What really harpooned Social Security was the false belief that there would always be more people working and paying money in than those people who are retired and drawing money out. You remember — the Ponzi scheme. Certainly by this juncture, you are more than familiar with the exponential growth concept by which we live and breathe. That plan is experiencing some technical difficulties. Technically, we're running out of money.

I think everyone knows who the baby boomers are. If you don't, let me assure you that there are a *lot* of them. Say, 78 million or so. In 2011, the first wave of the baby-boom generation will be eligible for full retirement. Between 2011 and 2030, it is projected that the number of people eligible for old-age benefits will increase by 80%. During the same time period, the number of people *paying in* to Social Security taxes will increase by about 2%.

Let's do the math on...nah, why waste good paper? That dog won't hunt. At the same time that this humongous group of people retire, they will also start to depend heavily on Medicare. Uh-oh, this isn't looking real promising.

So now we know what the future has in store for our government — and us — concerning funding Social Security and health obligations. If we couple that knowledge with a shrinking work force and continued heat for closing down the borders in a country where growth is the only thing that keeps us afloat, what will happen? I believe that after a short deafening silence, I just heard several quiet murmurs of disbelief, saying, "It won't work." That's what I've been trying to tell you — it won't work.

As gloomy as the scenarios presented for Social Security and Medicare are, the predictions for lasting even *that* long are projected on what? You guessed 'er Chester — economic growth. "How in the world are we going to have economic growth if the working population is going to be shrinking, half the country is on Social Security retirement and Medicare, and immigration is cut back?" If you can solve that riddle, information of that type would be extremely valuable to G.M. and Ford.

We do need to..."Hold it right there, wait, stop. If all these people are going to be retiring and scaling back, won't that eventually slow housing down and create a glut of larger homes on the market?" Yes it will. We should probably talk about that. We'll make it a point to do so, but first we need to talk about Medicare.

If Social Security were a problematic flu, then Medicare would represent a pandemic of stellar proportion. The future projections for the long green that will be required to fund Medicare make problems with Social Security seem a mere inconvenience. I believe that the rising cost of medical care is the second-largest problem in this country (right behind the idea that growth is the answer). If a middle-aged person is earning the minimum wage in 2006, their *entire* GROSS annual income would not cover the cost of a decent medical insurance premium!

Think about that statement. A minimum-wage earner makes a *gross* annual income of $10,712, or $892.66 per month. A quality health insurance plan for a middle-aged couple can easily exceed $1,000 per month. Like I said, even

Government Math folks have their limitations. So why don't "They" do something about it? Do me a favor, walk into the bathroom and look square in the mirror. That image looking back at you is one of "They."

Medicare is predicted to be insolvent by 2019; I don't believe that is accurate for many reasons. My opinion is that it will happen sooner. There are approximately 46 million people in the United States who currently do not have health insurance. This is equal to the *total* of ten states with the population of Colorado. Some states, such as Texas and New Mexico, currently report uninsured numbers of greater than 20% of their entire population.

Health insurance costs continue to outpace wage growth and the financial ability of most U.S. companies to pay the workers' premiums. Thousands of employees are being laid off (permanently) from high-paying jobs (refer back to G.M., Ford, Delta Airlines, etc). Health care premiums and rising pension costs are the most often-stated barriers to competing with foreign countries. In an effort for business to offset health care costs, more and more of the premium is being shifted to the workers, who then often elect to drop the insurance and buy food and clothing instead.

As more and more people *literally* can't afford health insurance, the premiums rise for those remaining who can afford to pay...to a point that another group drops their insurance and the cycle is repeated. More than 1 million *additional* Americans are going without health insurance each year. This trend has remained steady since the year 2000 and there is no reason to believe that it will not continue. So how can a problem that is this serious not receive the full and undivided attention of our fearless leaders? I'll set the stage to answer that question.

If you were on a cruise ship with a large group of people, all having a wonderful time, and a radio report came across announcing that another cruise ship in the area had sprung a leak in the hull, you would probably become somewhat concerned, after which another round of drinks would be ordered by the cruise director.

Now, if the captain of *your* cruise ship came on the radio and announced that *your* ship had a serious leak in the hull and was sinking, concern would be somewhat heightened and the cruise director would order a round of life jackets in the midst of a full-blown panic. "So what do sinking ships have to do with health insurance?"

Pretend that all the people on the ship who are being served cocktails have health insurance, and all the people on the sinking ship don't. We also need to pretend that the people on the cocktail ship are all Big Business executives and Federal Government leaders. You see, the people on the latter ship have health insurance and a wonderful pension plan. Their ship isn't sinking — yet. Unfortunately for the rest of us, those who potentially could have solved this known (known for 50 years) problem, have no personal interest in doing so.

I'm no fan of Big Business leaders or politicians (I know that comes as somewhat of a surprise), but the real truth is that they avoid the subject of health care like the plague, because there is no easy answer. Politicians love quick and easy solutions. A history of adopting hair-brained solutions for solving difficult problems is why we are in this mess to begin with. Dealing with difficult issues is especially dangerous around campaign time; and that is *all* of the time.

I repeat my belief that right behind "growth is the answer," healthcare is the most critical issue facing this country today. At the same time, we see U.S. companies moving their operations abroad on a weekly basis, citing their reason for doing so as the high cost of doing business in America. It only makes common sense to conclude that adding the cost of solving America's health care problems to Big Business's checkbook will certainly result in greater numbers of American jobs moving offshore.

The heads of G.M., Ford, and Daimler Chrysler met with President Bush in November 2006 to discuss their inability to fund health care at its *current* levels, and at the same time, compete with foreign nations. Pandora's Box was opened with NAFTA and the WTO, and we can't close it now.

I have read many articles that tout the virtues of the medical systems in Sweden, Canada, Germany, and other countries that offer national health care. It would be nice to say that a perfect model exists, and all we have to do is adopt it. But, it doesn't. Some may on the surface appear to be good solutions, but don't look too close. As an example, if a person had no preconceived ideas whatsoever about communism, and read Friedrich Engels' and Karl Marx's *Communist Manifesto*, you may come away believing that you had just stumbled onto a great idea. Communism touts the virtues of "all for one and one for all" — wow, what a concept.

There is a little problem with the "all for one" plan. Human nature spoils the day. I know that this doesn't happen at your house, but you have probably heard your friends complain about issues with Thanksgiving dinner. Not the food, the work. Some people buy the food, cook the food, serve the food, clean up the leftovers, do the dishes, and reassemble the wreck after everyone goes home. In Karl Marx's practice, they would be the communists. Some people watch the game, eat the food, make a mess, watch another game, eat some more food, make another mess, and go home. They are the communist leaders. I would wager that you have also worked with a few people over the years that have adopted another form of communism. You work, they don't; you get paid, and they get paid. Basic human nature can be a fierce foe.

Each of the countries that have implemented "all for one and one for all" health care have their own particular problems with maintaining status quo — mostly in that they *can't* maintain status quo.

Sweden has health care for one and all; they also have the highest taxes in the world and more problems than you can shake a stick at. Most of the world's countries that have cradle to grave social services also have vast disparities in the level of care between the social elite and the remainder of the population. They also share exorbitant taxes, a high incidence of alcoholism, elevated suicide rates, and diminishing government coffers.

The fact is, health care is a global problem and not one with an easy or existing answer. It is unlikely that a massive change will occur in the United States any time soon, even with the knowledge that the Medicare system will soon tip over. So what are we going to do? Depending on "They" to come up with something isn't the answer.

As we go forward from here, we are going to start relying a whole lot less on "They" and a whole lot more on the person that you see looking back at you in that mirror. "They" don't really have your best interests at heart, do they? *The government solution to a problem is usually as bad as the problem.* — Milton Friedman

PEOPLE AND PROFITS

FROM THE BEGINNING OF CHAPTER 1, we have continually looked at the known economic barriers that we face in the
coming years. We have also talked about the quick fixes that
have been applied to keep the economic train on the tracks. A
person with the awareness that all of my good readers now pos-
sess (sorry I did that to you) would have to ask, "How did we
ever let this mess get to this point?" Obviously, the origin of the
base problem was setting sail in a leaky boat called the *U.S.S.
Growth*. As to why we didn't come to grips with it sooner? That
problem goes back to the time when profits became more important than people.

We need to consider the true impact on our lives and those
of our children that have resulted from profits becoming more
important than people. Okay, if you're 95, maybe not, but give
some consideration to the 80 year olds. I'm not sure that the
quest for profits can ever be reversed. It is a standard that most
Americans believe in, heart and soul. For now, it is important to
understand *why* major companies behave as they do, in order
for all of us to live the best life possible, while we are hanging
around making profits.

Any life-changing event that unfolds over a long period of
time has the effect of becoming normal to us. Remember the
science experiment where a frog is put in a pan of cold water
and the heat is slowly, slowly turned up? The frog doesn't notice
the gradual increase in temperature, and gets cooked before he
jumps out. Well, your posterior has been warming up for years.

First though, we need to agree that the central theme for
planning any broad-based business venture should include the

analysis of both *sustainability*, and the *benefit* that it will provide *people*. When I say "benefiting" people, I'm talking about *all* of the people, not just the CEO and the Chairman of the Board. Agreed? Most Big Business today is aimed at profits first and people second.

Hold on to the belief that *all broad-based economic activity should have as its foundation the benefit that it provides to all of its people*. Think hard about what I'm saying. Profits must come second in importance to people, or we have totally missed the point. And right now, they don't.

In the book *Built to Last: Successful Habits of Visionary Companies*, by Jim Collins and Jerry I. Porras, they determined that companies whose core values held greater importance for their employees and the quality of their products, than that of profits, were ultimately the most successful and longest enduring companies in the United States.

Unfortunately, many corporate leaders have either failed to read *Built to Last*, or subscribe to the "take the money and run" management philosophy. When IBM froze its pension plan in early January 2006, thousands of its employees were a little put out, to say the least. That must have really gone bad for the CEO, huh? Not so much as you could tell. At age 65, his *retirement* income will be more than $10,000 *per day*. And that is, of course, seven days per week. Why? He is rewarded for making the company more *profitable*, regardless of the consequence to the employees.

Raking off profits to the top players is what Big Business is about. The CEO of Home Depot, Robert Nardelli, had reported total earnings in 2004 of around $14,000,000. Yes, as in *million*. That is a cool $38,356.16 per day, 365 days per year. I don't think that includes the personal jet service. In January 2007, Mr. Nardelli resigned as a result of falling stock prices and pressure from disgruntled stock holders. His severance pay for doing a bad job? $210 million!! "Outlandish, preposterous, outrageous, contemptible," you say? All that and more, but true all the same.

If a company produces a machine that replaces twenty workers, it is described as "ingenious, inventive, productive, progressive," and other glowing words that sound better than "for more profits." The twenty replaced workers are then described as "unemployed." But, it's ultimately good for them. "John, the company has just purchased a machine that will replace you and nineteen of your co-workers. Unfortunately, your services will no longer be required. The good news is that you will now be able to purchase the products that you were making prior to today for a much lower price, once you find another job." Now you can see where John and his nineteen unemployed colleagues would celebrate half the night, knowing that their loss is a huge benefit to mankind. And then again, maybe not.

We are constantly reminded that technology is beneficial to our lives. Robots that can do the work of ten people are nothing less than the cat's meow. American industry is absolutely transfixed on constantly replacing workers with machines. Producing more goods (growth, growth, growth) with fewer workers is the ultimate goal. The pinnacle of this quest is a building full of machines and computers that produce goods without having to deal with any irritating workers. More profits due to no wages, no retirement benefits, no vacations, and no problems.

I should say, no problems for the heads of Big Business. Government leaders, on the other hand, have a whole new set of difficulties trying to keep the extended unemployment numbers down. That creates a little math conundrum. Business and industry want fewer people employed, and government *needs* more.

Ford Motor Company announced late in 2006 that 38,000 workers had agreed to buyouts and separations from the company in a move that is designed to improve profits. That's bad news, huh? The offsetting good news is that Wal-Mart is hiring greeters and truck drivers to haul Chinese goods at one-fourth the current wage of the recently liberated autoworkers.

Speaking of Wal-Mart, let's see where they fit in to the "people and profits" picture. Sam Walton built the world's largest company on a concept that included the slogan "Made in America." Sam Walton is dead, and so is his slogan. Today, Wal-Mart is the nation's largest importer of cheap foreign goods.

The world's largest company constantly defends the practice of pressuring manufacturers for lower production costs as being good for American consumers by providing lower prices. This practice is sometimes referred to as "the Wal-Mart squeeze." So what happened to Wal-Mart's "Made in America"? Simple — Americans can no longer afford products Made in America; not on Wal-Mart wages.

Americans can't afford American-made products! Let's see now: we are the richest nation on earth and we can't afford to purchase American-made goods, so...then, who can? You don't suppose that has anything to do with the current $725.8 billion annual trade deficit, do you? Nah, probably not; cheap foreign products are good for us. Judging from the fact that the Walton family has accumulated somewhere in the neighborhood of $100 billion in personal wealth, I'd have to say that it has been more than good for them. Remember that Modern Colonialism thing? It really is working isn't it? Profits at Wal-Mart are ultimately more important than people. But, remember — it's *good* for you.

Wal-Mart, while certainly not alone, is one of the most visible examples of forcing manufacturing businesses out of the United States. The adoption of NAFTA and the WTO made cheap imports available and Americans love a bargain, regardless of who loses their job (as long as it isn't theirs). As cash tightens due to skilled job losses, and average pay decreases in the United States, Wal-Mart is none the less, a cheap place to shop and finds new customers from the ranks of those who now have less disposable income as a result of loosing their jobs from the "Wal-Mart squeeze." By this point, they also have virtually squeezed the competition (who was selling American-made products) out of existence. Good plan for Wal-Mart, excellent plan for China, bad plan for America.

I don't want to stray too far off course, so let's quickly recap a few critical points from the earlier chapters. Why did we open the borders? Why is all this cheap foreign competition necessary? The answer: we were out of shoppers. Our economy will fall flat on its face without growth. *Domestic* growth at levels capable of sustaining our *present living standards* became impossible to maintain, so we opened up to the rest of the world.

It would be unfair to say that this undying penchant for profits is purely driven by greed. Our systems of free enterprise and capitalism have their down sides and, left unchecked, certainly promote practices that put profits well in front of people. Competition is a wonderful thing...to a point. Unfortunately, we passed that point some time back, if we consider benefits to people as being our chief focus on this adventure that we call "life." Notice that I didn't say that capitalism and free enterprise were *bad* things; I said "left unchecked," they contribute to greed, and greed is a bad thing, for sure.

Our founders knew all about runaway business, greed, and corruption. That is why we have laws that control monopolies, usury, price fixing, collusion, and so on. But, as time has gone by, the checks and balances have weakened, and the people lost out to profits.

How does free enterprise harm people? Say that you decided, many years ago, to make and sell cookies, and good cookies at that. Your cookies began selling like crazy and customers were buying all of those delectable treats that you could produce. To step up production, you hired more help. The cookie business became so successful that you built a big bakery and had oodles of people employed, who enjoyed their work making a top-quality product. Everybody was happy, right? Not even close to happy.

Someone noticed your success and determined that they would like to force you out of business, and transfer your current earnings to their future accounts by making cookies cheaper. (Wal-Mart had promised to stock the world's cheapest cookies.) So rather than having real people who personally take an interest in making good cookies, the competition realized that they could buy frozen cookie dough from communist China and a Taiwan cookie machine that presses, bakes, packages, and ships the cookies without ever being touched by human hands. This is called "modernization, globalization, high efficiency, and out of work" if you are the American cookie maker.

You see, if you can get the dang wage earners out of the picture, you have a winner for profits and a market at Wal-Mart. It probably doesn't surprise you that this practice for replacing workers with foreign-made machinery is not limited to cookies. So, has the ability in our example of being able to buy cheap cookies by replacing the workers with machines been a benefit to society? This practice has been applied to nearly every job in America, in an attempt to reduce costs and shed workers; but is that the best thing for the people? You're told every day that it is, and so it *must* be true. *Preconceived notions are the locks on the door to wisdom.* — Merry Browne

Now, don't get me wrong — I don't think *all* machines and advances in technology are bad. Refrigeration, modern transportation, food production, medicine, communications, and ice cream cones are examples of advancements that have made our lives better. On the other hand, a robot that can take the place of ten workers has made *profits* better. I have read long dissertations that presume to explain how the present movement to mass production machinery and the importation of cheap foreign-manufactured goods are beneficial to us. Here's what I propose: if the people who write those explanations would move to the country where they make the cheap foreign products, *that* would be even better for *us*.

All of these changes that we have been discussing are nothing more than weak attempts for trying to get a few more miles out of a dead horse. We can't expand our way to prosperity, regardless of how fast we go or how many machines we build. The changing business environment and the sudden urge that you feel to learn Spanish and Chinese are merely previews of coming attractions.

The constant fortification by government and business that growth will allow us to continue living at the standards that we currently enjoy is purely an illusion that is being projected in order to distract your attention while the water is getting hot enough to cook your behind. In the mean time, the Wally World Waltons are going to continue to enjoy the luxuries of the Great American Dream, but I don't really think they intend to invite you over for dinner.

The heat applied to constantly produce more products with fewer people was actually being turned up for a long time, and like the frog, we really haven't noticed. As American products became less able to compete globally, we compensated by going faster. Producing more products, with fewer people in less time was somehow sold to most Americans as a good idea. "A good idea for who?" is the question. A little published fact is that *Americans today spend more time at work than any other people on earth.*

Over the past 30 years, more and more women have entered the workforce, and the dual-career, two-person family income has become standard, if not necessary. Infants go to day-care centers in order for mothers to quickly return to work in an effort to maintain status quo in the bank account. Jet travel across the country and back the same day has become custom-ary practice to pace the new speed of business. Extended travel away from home and family has been accepted as part of the new high-speed economy.

Letters that cost $14.00 to guarantee next-day service is a standard expenditure. Computers that do the work of hundreds of humans fill our workplace and have propelled business to supersonic speed. Goods can be ordered in the afternoon from across the country and delivered by 10 AM the following day. Stress levels in the workplace have climbed to all-time highs in an effort to produce the instant results that are expected at every level. Laptops are carried like briefcases, and cell phones are worn as a seemingly permanent adornment to the ear in an effort to stay in contact with the speed of business at every waking moment. Fast-food is crammed in between and during calls, while stores are open 24-7 so that if we decide to shop at 2 AM, we're not inconvenienced. And all of this is considered NORMAL!

Had someone made these suggestions a few years ago, they would have been put somewhere where they could rest and hopefully get well. So, are all of these changes ultimately good for people, or profits? Personally, I think we've been snook-ered.

It is common news today to hear that a person wigged out and shot up their workplace and co-workers. Or that a kid shot up the school along with their classmates. I often hear the comment, "I don't know what has gotten into people today."

"Americans are dancing as fast as they can." I believe that the mind has *physical* limitations the same as the body, and therefore requires a given amount of rest to remain healthy. A case in point may be seen in athletes. New world records are not set each week. Gravity and the development of the human muscular system reach an impasse where higher and faster, for the most part, are no longer possible. So why wouldn't the mind have the same limitations? It does, and there is a natural rest period required that doesn't include a life that consists of 24-hour work and stress. Yet our economic system requires ever *more and faster* to accomplish the necessary growth. I see some of you are nodding your heads emphatically in agreement.

Going faster and producing more can't be a good thing for the majority of humans living in a world of finite resources, and more importantly, a finite lifespan. Doing so limits the ability of the masses to live simply. Farming is an excellent example. Not so many years ago, families earned a living on 80-acre farms. Today it could prove difficult to extract a living from 800 acres. Small business has given way to Wal-Mart and Kroger. Family life, child rearing, social interacting, and quiet enjoyment have been cast aside in favor of high-speed careers, for the inexplicable goal of accomplishing ever-greater production and profits. What's the trade-off? Nothing that important — only your life.

For those of you who still believe that going faster will work out for the best, you have probably read as much of this book that is necessary. From this point on, we're going to be hitting the brakes, not the accelerator.

CHAPTER 11

LIVING IN THE SYSTEM

AT SOME POINT, I BELIEVE that strong resistance will mount in those who do not wish to participate in the current supersonic system. Those who become unwilling to sacrifice core family values, friends, and reasonable leisure time find themselves in a precarious situation. To the majority of this growing group, changing the direction of the system to a more sustainable and family-oriented lifestyle seems hopeless. Yet, even to those who resign themselves to the belief that there is little hope for meaningful change, the *internal* resistance continues to mount. What happens when resistance continues to build? Just like the resistance to over-current in an electrical wire, the situation begins to heat up.

You don't have to look far to find someone writing about the coming of an organized vocal and violent revolution of the masses. Most of these writers theorize that there will be a revolution against the ever growing government taxation, the real or perceived unfair distribution of taxes, corporate corruption, and inequitable global trade practices.

For others, all of these troubling changes have just become "the way it is," and that group will simply conform to what is dictated. At the same time, I believe that there are several groups of revolutionaries that are already in full revolt, in the form of non-compliance. We see the kids with orange hair, nose rings, tattoos, and clothes that don't fit. While these kids may not fully realize what it is that they are protesting, this is a *visible* revolution against the system. Who knows, maybe these kids that have grown up watching television eight hours per day without either parent at home didn't like it. They may also have been watching the whirlwind lifestyle of their parents with the same intensity that they watched television, and decided not to personally partake in the current festivities.

The *invisible* resistance is yet another group of people all together. These are the people who said enough is enough, and *purposely* dropped out at some level. This group is the most damaging form of revolution to our present system, for it chips away at the very foundation of our "earn and tax" and "own and tax" system. Your income, home, auto, business equipment, business real estate, etc., is taxed in ever increasing amounts each year. The more you have, the more you pay — forever.

Say that you are a young working person with enough student loan debt to choke a large horse, and you are also about to get an inheritance from your parents that is comprised of their Medicare, Social Security, and National Debts. Let's also say that you have a firm grasp of basic math and a fundamental understanding of NAFTA and the WTO. "Take her up to warp speed, Scottie — we have to increase production." "She won't stand much more, Captain. She's shaking apart."

So, with the *published* knowledge that America's future financial burden will be too great for the younger generation to bear, what might many of them be thinking? "Excuse me, Captain; I believe I'll get off at the next galaxy!"

Thousands of people have consciously dropped out of this system — that is, the work-and-pay-your-taxes system. These people are still firmly involved in the tax supported public education, housing, food, and medical systems. As Americans, we are a charitable bunch, and have developed a welfare system that begs to be exploited. Having housing, education, food, transportation, and medical care is a virtual *right* in America, regardless of one's personal efforts to help themselves.

So are the rights to retire for life from an insurance settlement, be it from a bad back, spilling hot coffee on one's lap, tripping over a chair in a restaurant, or faking an injury on the job. All of these people are looking for a way to exit the system permanently. And, I might say, for many, it is working quite well.

As the numbers of Americans who choose these new paths of rebellion rise, the tax burden must be shifted to the remaining working and taxpaying populace. At some point, funding this imbalance will require tax collection at a level where dropping out will make more and more sense. Nearly every day, I talk with sane, level-headed people who express a desire to make major lifestyle changes in the general direction expressed above (dropping out at *some* level).

In ever-increasing numbers, productive people consider dropping out of society and even leaving the country, for less hectic and cheaper places to live, such as Mexico, Costa Rico, etc. Small business suffers daily economic body blows. I speak regularly with small business people who want to release their employees and close their businesses. The most common reasons given are diminishing profits, increasing liability, and the necessity of longer working hours. Once more, we are dancing as fast as we can.

While some Americans choose to leave the country to make their money go further, the majority of us are not proponents of abandoning lifelong friends and family. While we can't change the course of our economy at will, we can change the way that we live in that economy. To do just that, we need to examine the personal changes that each of us could make that would result in the greatest benefit to our individual situations.

To thoroughly research our options, we must rethink the very manner in which we conduct our daily lives, and then *act* on those findings in order to better our chances for a happy life and the possibility of that storied eventual retirement. This adjustment may be the most difficult hurdle of all. Time has a way of making even the ridiculous appear normal. Rethinking *why* we conduct our lives as we do, however, is the key to making changes for the better. Humans are creatures of habit and, good or bad, old habits are hard to break.

Considering where the benefit lies for any activity which we engage in during our daily routine is important to making meaningful change. Cause and effect can most often be translated to cause and benefit. I was recently listening to a Wall

Street financial analyst who made a statement suggesting that the only one who could mess up the stock market recovery was the Federal Reserve Board — by raising rates. He went on to say that he doesn't even know why the Fed exists. This is what we call "spin, half-truths, B.S.," and, prior to everyone getting so politically correct — lying through his teeth.

I'll translate his statement about the Fed. "If the Fed would leave interest rates at 1958 levels, it would run inflation up like a heat-seeking missile. I could then rake off millions in trading fees and flipping real estate during the run-up period and get out before all those other schmucks ever get the news." In the event that you are not in the envious position of raking off millions, consider yourself to be in the group referred to as "those other schmucks."

There will always be those who spend their *entire* lives conjuring up new schemes to rob you of your *entire* life's labors. This less-than-honorable group of people create illusions that appeal to our desire for instant gratification. In order to make meaningful changes in our daily lives, we have to see through the scam artists plans for involving *your* time and money in *their* future aspirations.

The psychology of the human mind is what makes the scam artist's grand scheme possible. Abraham Lincoln said, "You can fool all of the people some of the time; some of the people all of the time; but you cannot fool all of the people all of the time." "Honest Abe" was dead on with that statement, but it left the door wide open for "fooling most of the people most of the time," and for those in the fooling business that is a recipe for outstanding success.

The fooling business needs a couple of elements in order to reach maximum success levels, and humans seem to be more than up to the task of providing those elements: gullibility and stupidity. *Only two things are infinite, the universe and human stupidity, and I'm not sure about the former.* — Albert Einstein

For example, Mr. Gullible & Mrs. Stupid are shopping for a new car and the salesman says, "I can send you home today in this brand-spanking-new SUV for less than $50,000

($49,999.99). It has four-wheel drive (nearly mandatory in Miami and L.A.) and all the bells and whistles that will make your neighbors green with envy." (The only "green" we're talking here is the liberation of the couple's green for 60 months or so.)

The salesman continues, "We have seen this model get up to four miles per gallon with a good tailwind on a downhill grade, and the license plates will run you a paltry $1,100 per year. The sales tax will be slightly over $3,000, and the insurance shouldn't cost more than, say, $200 per month. Your first day depreciation can't possibly exceed $12,000. We can finance the entire amount, including license and taxes, and your payment for a short 60 months will be the low, low sum of $1,100 per month. By the time you get this baby paid off, it won't be worth spit. What do you think?" "You did say that you could finance the entire amount, didn't you?" "Absolutely, and we can throw in $2,000 cash back." "That's incredible! We'll take it!" Pretty funny, huh? Pretty true and pretty dumb is what Mr. Einstein would have said.

The car dealer doesn't really present the deal exactly like my example. It is exactly the truth, but unless the salesman came down with a sudden case of conscience, his version wouldn't even resemble the truth. If it did, a few people who had mastered elementary mathematical addition, may not buy the SUV. He *would* tell you about all the bells and whistles, the extended warranty program, and the untold enjoyment that you are going to extract from the ownership of that fine motor car. His claims are backed by the tantalizing ads on TV every night, and if it's on TV, it *must* be true.

An old friend once told me that there are two things that you can't talk a person out of: buying a new car, and getting married. He may have been right, but I'm going to try anyway — not getting married, the car! What is the real cost of a new car, and how do you benefit from buying one? The long-term cost of a new car goes far beyond the obvious and, it may be the second worst idea that you've ever had, next to the boat. "BOAT," by the way, stands for **B**reak **O**ut **A**nother **T**housand.

The benefits of purchasing a new car are numerous; they benefit the company that makes the car, the dealership who sells the car, the county who collects the sales tax, the state who sells the plates, the bank who collects the interest, the insurance agency who collects the premium, and…I guess that's about it. What about the benefit to the buyer? I suppose you could be proud of assisting the aforementioned beneficiaries' children with college tuition and, who knows, maybe a new car.

The real cost of the new car are all the items listed above, plus any cash that you may have to put down. I'm going to assume that if you are reading this book, you are probably not chumming around with the trust fund crowd, whereas you do not have an endless supply of O.P.M. (other people's money), which forces you to use your own money. And, in that case, there is a cost involved. "Loss of opportunity" is the loss that one incurs from tying up cash in a low or negative return situation. The following example should help you to determine just how costly a nice new car can be.

For our example, we are going to assume that our buyer is 30 years old, lives in an area that charges 6% sales tax, has no trade-in, and that the *total* purchase price of the new SUV is $36,000. We will also assume that our buyer has good credit, can get a 6%, 60-month car loan for the entire purchase price (including taxes), and has a good driving record for insurance purposes. The calculations are based on driving the car an average of 15,000 miles per year. Our buyer will pay the license plate fees and insurance premium with cash.

While each state varies, the license fees and insurance in our example are actual costs for western Colorado. Don't worry about it being a little more or less in your home state; the results are so horrible that it won't make any difference.

The following are the costs for the first year of ownership, including depreciation, which was taken from the *NADA Appraisal Guide* for a one-year-old SUV with 15,000 miles that sold new for $36,000.

2006 Chevy Tahoe 4X4

Purchase price	$36,000.00
	(after discounts)
Total loan	$38,160.00
	(including sales tax @
	6% = $2,160.00)

Unrecoverable costs:	
Sales tax @ 6%	$ 2,160.00
	(included in loan)
License plates	$ 800.00
1- year interest	$ 2,106.07
1-year insurance	$ 1,836.74
1-year fuel @17 mpg	$ 2,047.00
1- year maintenance	
(tires, service etc.)	$ 990.00
1-year depreciation	$ 6,350.00
	$14,129.81 = 1st-year
	total *unrecoverable*
	expense
1-yr. principal payment	
on loan.	$ 6,746.81
	$20,876.62 = 1st-year
	total combined cost
	and depreciation

As you can see, the first-year cost of owning a new SUV is somewhat staggering. From a cost standpoint, it would be nice if we didn't have to own a car at all, but I'm not going to suggest anything that drastic. I will instead compare the cost of buying a two-year-old sport utility vehicle against our example above.

It should also be taken into consideration that there are those individuals who don't mind working six days per week until 48 hours prior to their funeral and to whom, therefore, this example wouldn't apply. Let's face it, we do nutty stuff and then wonder what the heck happened.

We will use all of the same buyer criteria as stated above for our comparison. I'm going to keep you somewhat sporty with a 2004 Chrysler PT Cruiser, 4-door Limited, with 30,000 miles on it. Average miles per gallon is 23. Most lenders will only loan for 48 months on a used car, so that is the number we will use. Okay, if your reaction to the Cruiser was that it won't pull the boat, the snowmobiles, the ATVs, and the 32-foot travel trailer, we're singing out of different hymn books. Don't give up on all of those things, though; follow along, and you may just have an opportunity to own a few of those toys at a significant discount when your neighbor has his bankruptcy sale.

2004 P/T Cruiser

Purchase price:	$15,175.00 (NADA Appraisal Guide for 2006)
Total loan:	$16,085.50 (including sales tax @ 6% = $910.50)

Unrecoverable costs:	
Sales Tax @6%	$ 910.00 (included in loan)
License Plates	$ 213.70
1-year. interest	$ 865.33
1-year insurance	$ 1,360.34
1-year fuel 23 mpg	$ 1,513.04
1-year maintenance (tires, oil, service)	$ 780.00
1-year depreciation	$ 1,825.00
	$6,557.41 1st-year total *unrecoverable* expense
1-yr. principal payment on loan.	$ 3667.87
	$10,225.28 1st-year total expense

There are countless cars that I could have used rather than the PT Cruiser. We could have chosen a mini-van, pick-up truck, sedan, sports car, and so on, but the purpose of this exercise is not to suggest a particular car for you, but rather to illustrate what is financially possible by making this one change in an auto choice. You could pick a myriad of different cars that will fulfill your need, and that *need*, by the way, is transportation.

The difference in the first year total expense between the PT Cruiser and the Tahoe is a measly $10,650.60. Hardly worth mentioning, considering the additional enjoyment that one extracts from the sheer driving experience of a new SUV. However, let's assume for the moment that the buyer could have qualified for the Tahoe, but in some fit of reality decided on the Cruiser instead. Let's also pretend that retirement for our 30-year-old buyer is something that she or he would like to accomplish well before the embalming process.

What would happen if the difference in ownership costs over the five-year loan period of the Tahoe were invested? That would, of course, certainly depend on the investment. There are numerous mutual funds that have historically returned something north of 10%, but let's play fair and say 7% is the goal for our invested money over the long term.

We also need to determine what the beginning balance of our mutual fund account would be and what the monthly contribution into our fund would equal if we were to invest the exact monthly cost difference between our two example vehicles. This will vary over time, as our costs for the two cars will be different.

Before I give the example of an investment in a mutual fund, I need to make a disclaimer: I have grave doubts about the continued health of the general stock market. On the other hand, I am *positive* that a new car is a first-class loser, and a comparison is necessary to demonstrate just how bad that loss can be. I personally prefer *real* estate as an investment, with the emphasis on *real*. If you are investing in individual stocks or mutual funds, be very careful, and seek out honest, professional help from someone that you trust. It's *your* money! Now, with my conscience clear, let's look at the following example.

For our beginning balance, we need to determine how much additional *cash* it would take to put the Tahoe on the road, as compared to the Cruiser. That number is the difference between the cost of license plates and six months of insurance, which we paid up front, and, it amounts to $824.50. Rounded up to $825.00, this will be our initial deposit into a mutual fund.

I have divided the remaining out-of-pocket costs by twelve that will be spent for one year of operation for each of our cars, including the second six month insurance payment, to determine the monthly difference in cash outlay. These costs include the car payment, insurance, fuel, and maintenance. The difference in these costs is $441.82 per month.

That is the amount, then, that could be deposited each month into our mutual fund account. Since the Cruiser can only be financed for 48 months rather than 60, it will be paid off a year earlier. So, during the last 12 months of our 60-month comparison, the Cruiser will be paid off, and we can include the former payment in our mutual fund investment, bringing the amount that can be invested up to $819.59 per month. Keep in mind that we are investing *exactly* the same amount each month for both auto owners.

At the end of the 60 months, the Cruiser will admittedly have 105,000 miles on it, but our mutual fund account will admittedly have earned $30,334.38. The residual value of the Cruiser will be about $4,442.00. Your total reward for forfeiting the smell of a new SUV and being the envy of the neighborhood is the residual value of your Cruiser, plus your mutual fund account value, or a total of $34,776.38. The residual value of the Tahoe with 75,000 miles on it will be near $17,075.00, and there is no mutual fund to calculate. Subtracting the residual value of the Tahoe from the combined residual value of the Cruiser and the mutual fund balance is $17,701.00.

As we can see from this example, not being quite so cool is worth $17,701.00 over the life of the SUV payments. If you were to take the residual of the Cruiser ($4,442.00) and put it down on a *one*-year-old car with 15,000 miles on it, you could repeat the same process, but the growth of your savings would be a little higher. After a total of 10 years (from the beginning of our example), the second car would be 6 years old with 90,000 miles and a residual value of approximately $6,000. The mutual fund would have now have earned $79,315.51.

What would happen if we continued to deposit the money in the mutual fund at our present level and traded cars every five years until our original 30 year old buyer was 60? Our mutual fund would have earned $584,554.47, and all the while, our two buyers would have driven the same amount of miles, just not quite as cool.

I know that I have stirred up a hornet's nest with all these figures that make way too much sense. I also know that some of you are saying, "Hold on, I have a warranty on my new car, and you can't compare a used model without considering repairs." No, I can't, and neither did the manufacturer. How many times did you take your last new car in for *major* repairs in the first two years or 30,000 miles? The answer for most new cars is none.

But more importantly, if the two year old car in our example had experienced a major problem in the first two years, the original owner of the car would have taken it in and had it fixed! After that you are on the same footing as any other two-year-old car owner, with the noticeable difference over the original owner of having several thousand dollars *in* the bank rather than *owed to* the bank.

When we bought our two-year-old car, it still had 6,000 miles of transferable warranty remaining. That gave us more than ample time to determine whether or not the car had a problem. If a car doesn't have major problems within the first two years, the odds are good that it will run beyond any warranty that the manufacturer offered to begin with. Why do you think dealers offer low-cost extended warranty? It's because the items that a warranty covers rarely fail. The argument about warranty being the reason for buying a new car is as old as the first car salesman who said it was so. And that was a long time ago.

Remember when you were thinking about the Cruiser not pulling the boat, snowmobiles, ATVs, and the 32-foot travel trailer? A new automobile is a first-class investment compared to buying new Big Kid toys. The first-year loss on this category of possessions that make you poor...I mean happy...would make a grown man cry and a kind woman kick her dog. That is, if it weren't for the joy that one perceives...I mean, receives, from those horrendous losses. These wonderful assets (ha-ha) drop in value like Enron stock.

If all of these fun Big Kid toys (including new cars) are such losers, why do so many people buy them? I'll try and be as kind as possible here: they buy them because they think new toys are going to make them happy. That being said, if working full time until you are 85 makes you happy, new Big Kid toys are a mortal cinch to insure that your aspirations of a long working life come true. "So?" you ask, "Why don't the really smart shoppers buy these toys for half price after the first owner declares bankruptcy?" That is a very good question.

People don't buy used merchandise for bargain prices, because the sellers want at least a small amount of cash. "Come again?" Sure, the seller wants cash, like in real money, before you can take their half price merchandise home with you. The problem is that the average red-blooded American consumer doesn't have any — any cash that is. They do, however, have credit. Ah-ha, now we are getting to bottom of this lunacy. Most Americans are so stretched out financially that they have no cash — as in *nada*. **Therefore Americans buy things that they don't need, with money that they don't have, borrowed from people who understand compound interest.**

If you go to the bank and ask to finance a new car, the bank will finance up to 107% of the sales price in order to cover the vehicle cost *and* the plates and taxes. But, if you are a smart consumer with good credit and want to buy a two-year old car at a bargain, the standard lender policy is to lend somewhere around 75% of the actual vehicle cost, and you are on your own for the 25% down-payment and the plates and taxes.

In our previous example of the purchase of a new SUV, if we take the first-year depreciation into consideration, the consumer owes more than the car is worth when they drive away from the dealership. If the lender were to encounter the unfortunate necessity of having to repossess that car in, say, six months, they would take a loss of somewhere around $5,000.00. On the other hand, if a repossession of our PT Cruiser (or whatever used car you chose) were necessary, the lender's loss would be about $1,000.00.

So, now you can see why banks loan higher percentages on new cars than two-year-old cars; they thrive on risk. Not really; they like business, and to get business, one has to compete. In this case, the banks and credit unions have to compete with the new car manufacturers who will gladly finance your new car for zero down and from 0% to 2.9% interest, if you have good credit and will take their deal. Their deal is that you pay enough for the car to make up for the illusion of 0% interest.

In the car business, you can have it one of two ways: your price and their terms, or your terms and their price. Note that you may *not* have *your* price and *your* terms. Back to the lender: even though it makes no financial sense whatsoever, the only way the banks and credit unions can compete with Chrysler Credit, Ford Motor Credit, G.M.A.C., etc., is to offer the same kind of deal the manufacturer offers. The advantage to the buyer, even though they may pay slightly higher interest to the banks and credit union, is that they can make the best deal possible with the car dealer and normally finance less money. In the end, the bottom line remains the same — you just lost your shirt.

"So then, why do banks and credit unions ask for higher down payments on late model used vehicles that are far less risk?" Because they don't have competition from the manufacturers, who have no interest in financing used vehicles. In fact, if the manufacturer had anything to say about it, all vehicles more than two years old would have to be sent to China.

The same lending policies go for snowmobiles, motorcycles, boats, and so on. The manufacturers need growth, and if they have to extend 100% credit to sell their product, that's exactly what they are willing to do. There are some things in life that just don't make sense. The statement, "cash is king," is oh-so-true. Having cash money for a down payment to take advantage of a bargain will save you untold thousands of dollars and, more importantly, untold days that you won't spend at work, earning money for the pleasure of paying interest.

In our comparison on the Tahoe and the PT Cruiser, I financed 100% of both cars, including taxes, to make an accurate comparison of costs. Had we put money down on the Cruiser, it would have made an even bigger difference in long-term savings.

Albert Einstein said that compound interest was the greatest mathematical discovery of all time. Lenders would certainly agree. Lenders are also nearly ecstatic over the continual reports that student math scores in the United States are on the decline. That gives them some reasonable assurance that most people will continue to pay interest without ever considering that it is not a mandatory expense.

If a person plans properly, having the trappings associated with success may appear to come easy, but "smart" and "easy" are sometimes confused along these lines. *Those who understand compound interest are destined to collect it, and those who don't are doomed to pay it.* – Unknown

So, the next time your neighbor or sister-in-law stops over to show you their brand new SUV or boat, instead of saying, "WOW, is that nice, or what?", you can say, "WOW, are you stuuupid, or WHAT?" Maybe you shouldn't say that; you may want to borrow it sometime. After all, there's no use in both of you having one.

THERE'S HOUSING, AND THEN THERE'S HOME

"HOME IS WHERE THE HEART IS." Sounds like a picture from grandma's kitchen. I have always cherished that statement. But then, I cherish most things that are simple, true, and deal with the real reasons for hanging around on this planet. The words "home" and "house" have somehow been convoluted. Actually, I shouldn't say *somehow* been convoluted, because that would suggest that I don't know how it happened. I think I just heard someone say, "Get ready, he's going to tell us whether we want to know or not." And I am. It's for the same reason that people drive cars that look like small apartments. The incessant advertising associating the rich, famous, and apparently successful with fine homes has done the trick.

Most of us want to be rich, famous, and successful to some degree. At least we would like to give that appearance to our friends, neighbors, and in-laws. Hopefully the people at the mortgage company aren't our friends, because they know that we aren't rich, suspect that we aren't famous, and are sure we aren't bright. But, with any luck, they will keep that to themselves. We commit many of our financial blunders purely from practicing normality.

I know it's difficult to be rational after committing years to the necessary practice of irrational behavior in order to appear normal, but at least give abnormal behavior some consideration.

How many of you have had someone tell you that a home is the best investment that you will ever make? Uh-huh, everyone, and from the enthusiasm displayed, everyone believes it to be true beyond any need for further discussion. But I'm not going to let you off that easy. Home builders and mortgage lenders will tell you about the virtues of home ownership all day and twice on Sunday, and they aren't lying. For them, it's a magnificent investment. In fact, the bigger the home, the better the investment for the builders and money lenders. If our homes were true investments, we could hang around the house and watch the money roll in rather than roll out.

In actuality, a large and glamorous home is similar to a large and glamorous SUV. The beneficiaries of the dollars spent on it are the builder, the tax collector, the utility companies, the insurance company, the maintenance companies, and the lender. Nearly everyone benefits more than the proud owner. I suppose the homeowners could take some pride in their role of helping all the aforementioned live a more flamboyant lifestyle. Spreading the wealth is a great thing in America, and nothing spreads the wealth quite like 30 or 40 long years of extra-large house payments.

Yep, I did say *40* years. It used to be 30 years max, which was dumb, but in June of 2005, Fannie Mae (secondary mortgage buyer) passed way beyond dumb and began buying *40-year mortgages* (as in a 280-year-old dog's life). The secondary mortgage market realized that some of the new home buyers needed a little more time to make the payments if the real estate express was going to remain on time. Therefore, a 40-year instrument graciously made it possible for young buyers to pledge the remainder of their working lives to purchasing a home. Great deal, huh?

It is *huge* for any U.S. President to tout that a higher percentage of Americans (with dropping math scores) are obtaining home ownership on his watch. Do you know that 50-year loans are now possible? The good old "Half Centurion" is available. Why *not* a 50-year mortgage? We need the G word, and regardless of the damage done to our future generations, we're going to get it. "Elect me for growth, growth, and more growth." Amen.

When interest rates become low and repayment terms become long, it creates higher home prices due to increased affordability and demand. However, housing isn't instant and new subdivision approval and infrastructure is some two years out. This creates the appearance of a shortage, and temporarily, that is true. A brisk market and heavy demand coupled with a temporary shortage in a capitalistic society will always drive up prices. In concert, the rising prices soon erode the average person's ability to qualify. Wages cannot be increased to pace the new housing prices without sending inflation through the roof.

We know what happens to sitting politicians when inflation gets out of hand, don't we? They become sitting ducks for the opposition to pick off. So when housing gets out of reach for the average person, what can be done? Decrease the interest and increase the time for repayment. Backing a 40-year mortgage and at the same time questioning why Americans don't have savings is unconscionable, even for our Federal Government.

Earlier we talked about the majority of people's inability to comprehend time, as it pertains to the upright and breathing portion of our lives (my personal favorite period). We're talking **30, 40,** or **50** YEARS here! That's three or four dogs ago! We have GOT to talk seriously about this so-called "investment," which takes the majority of your adult life to pay for.

What the mortgage company really needs to say at closing is, "You have been found guilty by a jury of ad executives, home builders, real estate agents, and mortgage lenders of wanting to purchase more house than you can afford. Therefore, this closing company has no alternative other than to sentence you to 40 years of hard labor working at a job that you really don't like, in order to make timely mortgage payments for the remainder of your natural life."

Buying a large upscale house is a good investment, right? After all, it is your *home* and darn sure worth working your rear end off for 30 or 40 years to achieve partial ownership. Yes, *partial* ownership. No one in the good old U.S.A. actually ever *owns* their home. Try not paying your ever-increasing property taxes, and you'll quickly realize that you have a partner. As you may well know, when you don't pay your taxes, your government partner sells your house on the courthouse steps.

How can I put this subject in a context that won't hurt anyone's feelings? I'll be sensitive and just say that taking out a

30- or 40-year loan is the dumbest thing that you'll ever do, next to parachuting out of a perfectly good airplane.

Think about all that we have discussed for just a moment. Interest rates on savings are so low that's it's a joke. Savings in the United States dropped into negative territory in 2005 for the first time since 1933. Mortgage loans, even with artificially low rates, only work for the majority of new borrowers when offered as interest-only, 3- and 5-year adjustable rates, negative amortization (I love that one), and 40-year terms. THINK about what I have just said! The risk involved with these types of financing vehicles is not something that a reasonably sane person should volunteer to participate in. Not at this point on our economic roller coaster.

Before you run your book through the shredder, I know that I promised in Chapter 6 not to recommend a canvas house. I'm holding to my promise, and we are *going* to buy a *home*. However, for those who wish to ignore the following information due to your suspicion that it is being provided by a madman, a canvas house could eventually appear as an upgrade to living with your in-laws. We need to discuss the difference between a house, a home, and an investment; they aren't even close to the same animal.

A house is something that you live in, an investment is something that you live on, and a home is a house where you feel *peace* and *contentment*. It is much easier to feel peaceful and contented in a home that is paid for. Trust me on that last statement.

Relentless advertising and peer pressure — yes, adult peer pressure — cause us to do some really foolish things. We see our friends, co-workers, siblings, and in-laws buying houses that rival the Taj Mahal. Your mother-in-law starts dropping subtle hints such as, "I tried to tell my daughter not to marry a loser like you, but did she listen? Nooo. Her sister is living in a 4,000-square-foot custom at The Oaks Country Club of Pascagoula, and YOU are living in a TRACT home! How do you think it makes our family feel to see our daughter end up with a bum like YOU!" To which you answer, "Is it really possible to get a 40-year mortgage?" Dumb, dumb, dumb.

And to think, you told your kids not to smoke just because the other kids were doing it. I can still hear my dad saying, "WHY did you do that?" I would murmur not an answer, but a question, such as, "Because the other kids were doing it?" Dad's standard answer was, "If the other kids jumped off a cliff, would you jump, too? Do you think that thing sitting on top of your shoulders is for the single purpose of growing hair?"

Consider being sentenced to 30 or 40 years of hard labor before you commit the crime — of signing the mortgage, that is.

We discussed the reasons that housing exists at all in Chapter 6. It provides shelter, climate control, and a dishwasher. No more, no less. Subjecting yourself to a 30-year mortgage based on what your sister-in-law did just doesn't make much sense. Having time to enjoy our lives and having a little extra money for some simple pleasures seems a whole lot more appealing in the long run. Everyone should certainly own a home if at all possible, but let's do that in a manner that suggests some forethought.

The insanity of the "maximum possible loan" syndrome usually begins with the lender, who pre-qualifies buyers and arms them with a number that represents the highest amount that they are qualified to borrow, for the longest period of time, at the lowest interest rate achievable — normally, an interest rate that is subject to change, as in *adjustable*.

Longer terms and lower down payments are evident in nearly every sector of our economy, a definite sign of the times. Auto loans on new vehicles not so many years ago were limited to 36 months. Today, it is possible to get an *84-month* auto loan. Renting furniture and televisions with a small down and weekly payments is common. Dumb, but common. Why have these loan terms and conditions been continually altered? Costs, and the desire to own countless nonessentials, have outrun wages. Most Americans have little or no savings. There is no possible way that we can borrow our way to maintaining our present spend-more-than-we-make lifestyle. That would require growth beyond physical limitations. As the saying goes, this is "where the rubber meets the road."

Back to our potential home buyers, who are now out of the lender's office and off to the local real estate store, where the agent asks them what they are qualified to borrow. The buyer informs the agent that they can qualify for a 40-year adjustable rate mortgage of $250,000. The real estate agent then loads our prospective couple up in the car and shows them homes costing between $300,000 and $400,000, after which they show our excited couple a home for $250,000, which they don't like because the $400,000 house had a pool. The agent then suggests that they may want to consider borrowing the extra money needed from a relative, obtain a second mortgage, or sell one of their children to the slave traders; all of which seem reasonable alternatives if there is a pool in the balance.

So, our buyers, wanting to show up the Sister and brother-in-law, stretch their finances razor thin and get into the "pool house," as they now refer to their new source of eternal happiness. Eternal happiness? I think not. It will, however, buy "eternal moneyless."

That is the way that buying a house works, isn't it? We want the most house for the most money that we can possibly afford. It really is a human-nature thing. Euphoria rules supreme for just long enough to sign the mortgage papers. Joyous, mind-altering thoughts such as, "I love this home, it is the answer to complete and total happiness, regardless of cost," make us put pen to mortgage. Of course, they do. Just like the new car sensation did last year, the smell and euphoria are gone long before the payments are getting warmed up.

It becomes a terrible surprise to the new homeowner that the new house has many similarities to the old house. It needs cleaned, the windows need washed, the lawn needs mowed, the bushes need trimmed, and the garage is the same perpetual mess as the old one. All the same things that you didn't like to do in the old house are present in the new house, except the new house is larger and requires much more time to accomplish all the things that you don't like to do. In the event that this is a first homeowner experience, the new buyers will also notice the absence of a landlord at such times when the water heater springs a leak or the furnace needs repair.

Most new home buyers are in debt up to their eyeballs. Married couples must both maintain full-time jobs to make the payments, including the rent on the big screen plasma TV next to the pool where they watch *Survivor* while eating on TV trays and sitting on rent-to-own lawn chairs. The rental furniture people are bringing a dining set over next week. Truth is certainly stranger than fiction. But it doesn't have to be that way.

I have the absolute pleasure of knowing people from all walks of life that I can call friends. My friends range from monetarily poor to ultra rich. Some of the finest homes that I have ever been invited into were small cabins in a peaceful setting, modest homes in a quiet neighborhood, and, yes, mobile homes where I was welcomed and warmed. I said *homes*, not houses. No amount of glitz and glamour, size or cost, can make a house a home. Try as you may, it can't be done.

I think about my friends who live modestly and happily. When I arrive to the smiles and handshakes and comments such as, "Don't worry about your shoes, get in here out of that weather," I feel far more at *home* than when greeted with, "Please take off your shoes, we just had the two-inch white-pile carpet cleaned."

You can't buy a home, you can only buy a house. Not to wear this point out, but it is imperative to realize that size and stature won't get you where you want to go, unless you were already headed to the poorhouse. An affordable home radiates a warm welcome ambience that surrounds both the residents and the visitors, and *that* is where we are going.

The Biggest Lie Ever Believed is not just the title of this book. Giving up happiness, free time, and simple leisure in pursuit of a false promise and a large mortgage payment is a *terrible* trade. Debt is a way of life in America, and some debt is necessary to navigate our present economic system. But debt also rules our lives. Consider becoming debt free, and how different your life would be. Don't tell me that; of course you can do it!

You have heard or read a hundred times that the purchase of a house is the single largest *investment* that most people will ever make in their lives. For our purpose, let's change that to the purchase of a house is the single largest DEBT that most people will ever incur. To serve as a true monetary *investment*, a home would have to be sold in order to bring liquidity to that investment (real spending cash), not pie-in-the-sky equity. Selling your home in order to cash in on your investment could be a little inconvenient on cold nights. Living in the car can't be that much fun. Don't confuse debt and investment. Yes, you can borrow against your house to extract some cash, but then we would have debt and interest all over again, and we don't like debt and interest.

So, if high home debt is not a good thing, why has the American Dream continually grown in stature? Why have homes become larger, more grandiose, and unbelievably expensive? Because the American Dream is what holds up the American economy, and we know the American economy has issues. The Dream has gotten larger as the problems for holding this mess together have gotten larger. New home construction (as we have discussed) is the cornerstone of our present domestic economy.

The money made on development, construction, and tax collection is directly proportional to the cost of the home. Therefore, the higher the cost of the new home, the higher the profits for the developer, builder, real estate agent, and so forth. Government and insurance companies have a windfall all the way around: as the valuations of existing homes rise, so do the taxes and insurance. And who pays for all this wonderful commerce? The homeowner, of course — forever. Spending the majority of your remaining upright waking life working to pay for a house takes a little of the pizzazz off the whole home-sweet-home concept.

Here are a few of the common reasons that people use to justify high home ownership costs. "You have to live somewhere, why pay rent? Homes will always go up in value. We are going to use our growing equity to keep moving up. A home is the best investment that a person can make. You can write off the interest deductions on a home loan, but rent is just lost." The list is endless and the reasons vary, but most are fundamentally untrue. Home ownership is a wonderful thing if approached properly with truthful guidelines.

"Why pay rent." If you are *not* going to live in an area for a minimum of three years, rent is normally better than ownership. Ninety-five percent of the time, rent will be less than ownership on a true monthly expense basis. Costs incurred for the initial purchase combined with annual taxes, insurance, maintenance, and the eventual costs of resale will, in most situations, outdistance gains. There is also the risk that home prices will remain level, or even worse, decline in value. If this were the case, you could find yourself to be a very big loser when you have to sell.

In the meantime, the additional costs that would be going to home ownership can be socked away in a compound-interest vehicle, and provide a substantial down payment on a home in an area where you *do* wish to remain long term. I know that we have had an incredible rise in housing costs over the past several years, but I promise it won't continue; math won't let it.

Renting can also save money in areas that are not nearly as evident as those listed above. Furniture is a big one. Normally, when a person is going to be in an area for three years or less, they rent a smaller space than they would buy if preparing to stay put. That is less space to furnish, and less furniture to pack and move when the time comes. Furniture, once purchased, depreciates at about the same rate as a boat. In most cases, the value of common household furniture will fall below the cost to move it, let alone the hassle factor.

"We can write off the interest." This statement should be introduced into the "Misinformation Hall of Fame." Just think about it. To become eligible for an interest deduction on your taxes that will result in, say, a 25% reduction in what you finally pay, you must first PAY 100% of the interest to get 25% back! The actual math works something like this: 100% less 25% equals 75% of the taxes that you DON'T get back. What an incredible deal!

The belief that paying mortgage interest is a *good* thing has become so fully embedded in our mythical financial culture that many people truly believe that owning a home outright is a bad thing, due to losing interest deductions! Whoa! What part of this are we missing here? I know that you have heard someone (like your husband's cousin, Leroy) say, "Yeah, they just bought that big ol' place for a tax write-off." Now there are some tricky tax laws out there, and there may be some finagling by those with excessive income that appears to be suspicious, but, until the U.S. tax rates reach 101%, trust ol' Mike: paying interest to make money on a tax credit is barn broom dumb.

The confusion that resulted in the widespread belief that mortgage interest deductions are nearly mandatory for the live and sane is fairly simple: IF a person must pay interest, it is *better* (not to be confused with *good*) to pay interest on a *tax-deductible* debt, rather than a *non-deductible* debt. For instance, your home interest is deductible, your personal auto interest isn't. So, it may stand to reason that taking out a loan on your home for the purpose of buying a car (which you can write off), is better than taking a loan out on a car, which you can't write off. Even with this explanation, there is a small problem that is overlooked approximately 99.97% of the time. When you add a car to your house payment, you effectively agree to make car payments for the length of your home loan. If you think the car payment example that we looked at earlier is bad after five years, consider 30! I don't think the old buggy will run that long.

Interest is interest, akin to real money that you used to have, but don't have anymore. As in money that you could do something else with, such as starting a fire with a crisp, dry $100 bill, and get better value than seeing it go to most interest payments. So the next time one of your friends says they are taking advantage of an interest tax deduction, offer them the same deal that the Federal Government extends: they give you 100%, and you give 25% back. Yes, we all have to pay interest at some point, unless we have a generous aunt who will leave us her house and a nice little trust fund, but let's pay interest for the right reasons, not some phantom benefit from a tax deduction.

"Homes always go up in value." When I hear this statement, I think of people who have told me that once the temperature gets to 25 below zero, you really can't tell the difference when it gets colder. To fully believe this to be true, it is paramount to have never experienced 60 below zero. "What the heck does that have to do with home prices going up?" Anyone who says that homes always go up in value has never experienced homes going *down* in value — at least not *their* home.

I started this book by describing 1,200 vacant homes in the area where I was living in Alaska just after the inflationary building boom of the early '80s crashed. Going down in value is hardly a term that could vividly describe that period as it existed in much of the United States. I had a front row seat in that decline, and even I sometimes forget how devastating it was. Homes don't simply "always go up in value." Sometimes they go down. And, if you are connected to that decline with a razor-thin 30-year mortgage, you go down with it.

Over the long run, inflation has created somewhat of an illusion that suggests that homes continue to increase in value. Home prices do tend to pace inflation and, therefore, can act as a hedge against rising costs. But there have also been extended periods where home prices were either flat or in decline. The past years of upward home prices were induced by an increased money supply, record-low interest rates, longer mortgage terms, lower down payment requirements, and lower qualifying standards, which, in turn, have artificially pushed housing costs far beyond sustainable values in most areas of the country.

"We are going to use our growing equity to keep moving up." Good plan, but everyone else has the same one. Homes don't go up vertically, they go up laterally. In other words, everyone else's home goes up at the same time that yours does. When you sell, you can only buy a home equal to the one that you are leaving if you remain in the same area. Now, if your plan is to live in Aspen, Colorado, until you gain equity, and then move to Oklahoma when you retire, that plan may actually work. But then, now that I think about it, probably not. First of all, you aren't going to like mobile home living in tornado alley, and, second, if you could afford to live in Aspen in the first place, home equity is not all that high on your list of concerns.

What you *can* do by cashing in on your home equity is have a large down payment for a larger mortgage, in order to buy a larger house. Total sum gain = 0. Inflation wears many disguises.

"Homes are the best investment that a person can make." Absolutely true — if you purchase the right home, in the right place, at the right time, for the right reason, it can be the acquisition of a lifetime. But a home can also be the worst investment that a person can make if you purchase the home that most Americans buy. That is, once more, the most house, for the most money, for the longest period of repayment that they can possibly afford if everything in the next 30 years goes as planned. Heck, last week didn't go as planned, did it?

Without going into horrible minute details, we'll take a look at the real costs of home ownership. We need to set out a standard home deal (whatever that is) for our example. Home prices and markets vary so widely from region to region that our example may not fit your current area. However, the math is universal and equally fits New York, San Francisco, and Hong Kong.

Larger or smaller numbers are calculated with the same formulas. Some areas where homes have skyrocketed in value are far more dangerous and volatile to be sure, but that is not really the point here. How much of your working life you want to dedicate to *shelter* and how much unnecessary *risk* you want to assume, are the issues that we want to clarify.

For those of you who live in Santa Monica, California, or Aspen, Colorado, where the cost of an upscale doghouse exceeds the average home price in most of the remainder of America, the following example was not meant for you. But, if you do live in Aspen or Santa Monica, or their equally expensive counterparts, and are struggling daily to make your house payment and monthly living expenses: there are no border guards; sell out and get a real life in the sane portions of our country!

The perfect scenario for buying a home is to put down 20% and mortgage the balance with a fixed rate 15-year loan. I realize that many buyers don't have the 20% and, therefore, must settle for a lower down payment option, with a longer term in order to qualify. Qualify for what? The U.S. Olympic bankruptcy team? Think hard about what you are doing and what you are getting into. You're betting your remaining working life on it. The following example compares the costs associated with a 30- and a 15-year mortgage.

Our example house is a 1,575 square foot, 3 bedroom, 2 bath, ranch style with an attached double car garage in a residential subdivision. Few deaths have ever been attributed to living in a home of less than 3,000 square feet, even with a couple of kids. Our buyers have good credit, but want a low down payment in order to pay more interest for a tax deduction. In other words, they are typical buyers.

The price of our new or used home, whichever the case may be, is $200,000 (I know, I know, but this is just an example), and we are going to finance 97%, or $194,000, with an FHA loan for 30 years at 6.25%, which is good, because that is all the money that our buyers could get their parents to lend them for a down payment.

I realize that $200,000 doesn't buy much of a house in most of the United States today. I use this number as an example only to demonstrate the effect of time, money, and compounding interest. Had I used a higher cost home, the end result would have been far more dramatic.

The fact that our example buyers are only putting down 3% will require that they pay PMI, or Private Mortgage Insurance. "What in the world is this PMI stuff about?" I'm glad you asked; I was dying to tell you about it.

You see, the mortgage company doesn't have a whole lot of faith that they won't eventually be the new owners of a home that they just lent 97% of the appraised value on. They figure that between the new car and the rental furniture payments that there is a better-than-average chance that their new borrowers may come up a little short somewhere down the road. Since the borrowers' parents wouldn't agree to co-sign the loan, the lender wants a different kind of co-signer, called Private Mortgage Insurance.

This type of insurance helps protect the mortgage company against losses due to foreclosure. This protection is provided by private mortgage insurance companies and allows mortgage companies to accept lower down payments than would normally be allowed. This should give you some clue as to what you are getting into. The mortgage company is betting that you'll go broke and need backup.

Before you hear it from the mortgage company, you can also take out an additional higher interest loan and make a second payment, called a "piggy-back," to avoid PMI. What can I even say about a piggy-back, except DON'T DO THAT.

Private mortgage insurance also enables mortgage companies to grant loans that would otherwise be considered too risky to be purchased by secondary investors, such as our friends at Fannie Mae and Freddie Mac. The ability to sell loans to these investors is critical to maintaining mortgage market liquidity, which, in turn, allows mortgage companies to continue originating new loans, which, in turn, spells GROWTH. Without which, wall tents would soon come back into style as primary housing units. You can see the logic here, can't you? The new homeowner, who is already strapped and suspect for going bust, gets to pay an additional premium for PMI or a piggy-back loan to insure the house payment is made. I told you truth was stranger than fiction.

Back to our mortgage comparison. The principal loan amount for our example is $194,000, at 6.25% interest for 30 years, resulting in a monthly principal and interest payment of $1,184.33. The loan was initiated on January 1, 2006. I will add home insurance, taxes, and PMI using costs based on my home area in western Colorado. Real estate taxes will add $1,059.33 per year, or $88.27 per month. Homeowner's insurance will add $37.50 per month, and PMI will add an additional $147.12 monthly, bringing the grand total of principal, interest, taxes, homeowner's insurance, and private mortgage insurance to $1,457.22.

So what would happen if everything remained the same with the exception that our buyers elected for a 15-year loan? The first thing is that the interest rate would go down by about half of a percentage point, or 5.75%. The payment would then be $1,603.97. There would still be all the other costs as listed above, with the exception of PMI, which would be $129.00, or $18.12 less, bringing the monthly grand total to $1,858.74, or $401.52 more per month.

If our buyers were able to swing the difference per month in payments, let's take a look at what would happen. Okay, okay, I know that most homeowners today are not going to stay in the same home over the full term of the mortgage. Many home buyers use the excuse of getting a longer term mortgage due to having a plan for selling in five years, therefore the term doesn't matter, because they aren't planning on paying the house off anyway, and are simply going to sell and utilize the equity to move to a larger home.

Fair enough. That is a realistic situation in today's market. If our 30-year buyer were to sell after five years, considering that they had made the standard payment, the principal balance of the loan would be $180,900.89. They would also have paid an additional $8,827.00 for 60 months of PMI at the stated $147.12 per month premium.

If our 15-year mortgage buyer were to sell after five years under the same conditions, their principal balance would be $146,572.70. That would give our 15-year buyer $34,328.00 more equity over the same five-year period if neither home appreciated a dime. Yet the 15-year buyer made only $24,912.00 more in payments, so the remaining difference in equity between our two owners of $9,416.00 is interest. There is another savings for our 15-year owners: the savings in PMI would add another $3,022.00, making the overall savings and equity $12,438.00. You see, PMI is only required until the owner has a 20% equity in their home, and our 15-year buyer would have obtained that level of equity prior to the five-year payoff in our example.

Let's say that for some reason our buyers decide to stay put. As we discussed, it is only necessary to pay PMI until such time that a 20% equity is realized, or, for our example, until such time that the principal is reduced to $160,000. The 15-year mortgage reaches that level after 45 months of payments; the 30-year mortgage takes 129 months! No, you didn't read that wrong. It would take 10 years and 9 months to reach the same level of equity that would be achieved in 45 months on a 15-year mortgage.

While we are comparing the difference in these loans, once our 15-year buyer reaches the 45th month, the $129.00 monthly savings on PMI would reduce the monthly cost difference between a 15- and 30-year mortgage to $272.52. So what would be the difference in the loan balance at the time that our 30-year mortgage reached 20% equity? After 129 months, the principal balance on the 30-year would be $159,904.00. The 15-year mortgage balance would be $72,522.67! That is an equity difference of $87,381.33. But wait, there's more. Our 15-year owner hasn't been paying PMI since the 45th month of his loan. That would equate to an additional savings of $10,836.00 that was not paid out for PMI. The combined total of equity and savings on PMI is now $98,217.33. Oh, my!

The total cost to our 30-year owner for principal, interest, and PMI at 129 months is $175,323.48, as compared to our 15-year owner's $211,169.39 in total — a difference in out-of- pocket costs of $35,845.91. Yet the 15-year owner has $98,217.33 more in combined equity and savings on PMI. This calculates out to a benefit of $62,371.42 MORE than the actual cash difference that he paid out as compared to our 30-year buyer.

I'm really going to go out on a limb here and say that our 15-year buyer became so accustomed to paying PMI over the first 45 months, that he decided to apply the previous $129 PMI premium to the mortgage payment for the remainder of the loan. That would be pretty dumb, seeing that they are offering zero down and 0% interest on new SUVs, but let's pretend that our 15-year buyer graduated in the upper 90% of his sixth grade general math class, went completely loco, and made the extra payments on his home, instead of the new SUV.

To recap the situation, after 45 months, our 15-year buyer would reach 20% equity in his home, and could invest the

$129.00 that he was previously paying for PMI toward his mortgage payment. After the 129th month (when the 30-year buyer would be eligible to quit PMI), had our 15-year buyer applied the extra $129.00 each month without fail, his mortgage balance would be $59,626.60. Should our 15-year buyer continue to make the extra payment to the end of the loan term, his home would be paid off 13 months early, in November of 2019. Where would our 30-year buyer be? If we gave him the same benefit of converting his PMI toward the mortgage balance after reaching a 20% equity (129 months), he would still owe $138,409.34.

At the time that our 15-year buyer reached payoff, he would have paid $89,715.87 in interest and $5,805.00 in PMI, for a total of $95,520.87. At the same time, our 30-year buyer would have paid $150,921.54 in interest and $18,978.48 in PMI, for a total of $169,900.02, or $74,379.15 more than our 15-year buyer. Wow! But wait, I forgot to add that our 15-year buyer's home is now paid off, and the 30-year buyer still owes $138,409.34. So, at this point, our 15-year buyer has gained a total of $212,788.15 over his 30-year counterpart, and no longer has a house payment. "But their payment was a lot more," you say. Let's define "a lot."

Over the period of the loan, up to the payoff, we have determined that our 15-year buyer paid $95,520.87 in interest and PMI. He also paid $194,000 in principal during the same time period, resulting in a total cost of $289,520.00 over the length of the loan.

During the same period, we determined that our 30-year buyer paid a total of $169,900.02 in interest and PMI. They also paid $54,973.05 on principal, or a total of $224,873.07. The difference between our two buyers then was that our 15-year buyer paid out $64,646.93 more than our 30-year buyer over 167 months. That calculates out to a payment that was $387.10 more per month over the loan term, yet our 15-year buyer is $212,788.15 ahead at this point, or a gain of $1,274.18 each month, over the entire term of the loan. Seems impossible, doesn't it?

Okay, here we are with our 15-year buyer sitting pretty. He is now 44 years old (remember, he was 30 when we started). He has his home paid for and is wondering what to do with all his left over income. Our 30-year buyer knows exactly what to do with his income — keep paying interest.

I need to make a couple more points, and then we'll move on to the next chapter. I want to demonstrate how ugly a 30-year loan carried to term really is. To do that, we are going to follow our 30-year buyer to the end of term, when he will pay off his home. I can hear the discourse out there. You are saying, "No one pays to the end of a 30-year term." Maybe not on the *same* loan; but do Americans make cumulative mortgage payments for 30 years of their lives? Oh, yes — and then some. Many even take out second and third mortgages. The real costs of taking out *multiple* mortgages are far more punitive than the following example.

Setting the stage for the remainder of our 30-year buyer's loan term, we will continue to pay the $147.12 former PMI premium against the loan. At the point that we now reach pay-off (May 2032), our 30-year buyer will have paid $211,461.97 in interest and $194,000 in principal, or $405,461.97 total, plus $18,978.48 in PMI. That is a grand total of $424,440.45, and he now owns his home, three-plus years ahead of schedule, due to applying the additional PMI premium. Our 30-year buyer is now age 56.

In the meantime, our 15-year buyer has considered what he would do with his former house payment money and determined that he would save it in a tax-deferred retirement fund that averaged 7% return over the period that our 30-year buyer was continuing to make house payments. When our 30-year buyer pays his home off, our 15-year buyer's retirement fund will be worth $454,613.83. Our 15-year buyer is now acquainted with the process of collecting interest, and our 30-year buyer is acquainted with the process by which lenders drive Mercedes Benz sport coupes.

The 15-year buyer is also acquainted with the difference between a home and an investment, which is why he is $454,613 richer and, at the same time, has a home equal to that of the 30-year buyer. So what would it have taken to come up with the extra monthly payment for the 15-year loan? Let's assume, more realistically, that our buyers are a married couple. I can't begin to count the ways that a working couple could come up with the extra $387.10 per month, if they really wanted to.

Here are just a few ways that the extra money could have been accumulated. At a wage of $15.00 per hour, it would require 26 hours per month, or 6.5 hours per week — or, better stated, 3.25 hours per week for *each* person — to work a part-time job. A few less restaurant meals, not incurring credit card interest, and buying the things that you *need* rather than the things that you *want*, are just a few other ways on a list that could fill another book. In fact, I can easily produce realistic scenarios that would set our two example borrowers much further apart with an accumulation of $1,000,000 greater for the 15-year, over the 30-year buyers, rather than the $450,000 plus in our example. But that really would take another book, and, for now, I just want you to live better.

There are so many ways that the above scenario could change that I won't even attempt to calculate them. The math is real and the truth is evident. Some arguments would be that no one keeps a loan for 30 or 40 years. Or that the home will appreciate through inflation to the 20% equity level, eliminating PMI prior to the 129 months used in my example. Or, if a person could afford the payment on a 15-year loan, they wouldn't have taken a 30 to begin with. Or, a hundred more lame reasons that just don't hold water.

I could go on and on dispelling misinformation, but I reckon if you still want a 30-year mortgage by now, it won't do much good for me to continue beating that drum. Consider this, however: what if the house doesn't go up in value? What if it goes down in value? Now, there is a plot for a great horror movie, and one that is going to be showing soon in neighborhoods across this great nation.

It is no secret that there are 78,000,000 (as in *million*) baby boomers. Do you think as these people get older they will want larger two- and three-story homes? Do you believe that they will want to continue to incur the expense of hefty taxes, utilities, maintenance, lawn care, and the pool boy? Will they want to hike stairs in their older years? The answer to all of these questions is a resounding, "You gotta be kidding!"

So what will happen to the market for all these large homes? The generation coming after the boomers is smaller in numbers and tend to have fewer children. Take a wild guess at what the market will be for those mini-mansions that the boomers want to sell so that they can scale down. That market will be rougher than three days in jail. Not much of an investment, was it?

This current false market has given us an artificial sense of housing values. I believe that for most of this country, flat or declining home prices will materialize in the very near future. I also believe that this period in time may represent the most dangerous period of new home ownership since post-1946, especially for young buyers with marginal loans.

The flood of new homeowners, shepherded in by low-interest loans, is near to its predictable end. On the other side of any peak is a valley. In this case, I think the slope into the valley may represent a cliff. In many areas, I believe that it could take years for the false values in housing to correct to any semblance that would represent reasonable income vs. home price ratios. These are years that could be spent enjoying the good life, rather than struggling to hold onto a house that is worth less than the mortgage balance.

Marginal mortgages, such as inclining adjustable rate, negative amortization, and interest-only, are based on the premise that when the payment increases at a future preset time, the borrowers will be making more money and their homes will have increased in value. If you didn't start by reading this chapter first, you know by now that I believe such a scenario nearly impossible. Las Vegas seems a better bet, when you consider all that we have covered to this point. In every pitch for buying stocks, the caveat, "Past performance is not indicative of future gains," is included in the microscopic print at the bottom of the page or rapidly spoken at the conclusion of the vocal spiel. Real estate ads should contain the same caveat, but they don't.

In conclusion, a house, a *home*, and an investment are very different. Buy a home, not a house. Remember, a home provides shelter, not income. Don't devote the majority of your working life to paying for shelter only to realize that you were a victim of believing "The Biggest Lie Ever Believed."

Let your brain guide you, not your emotions. Euphoria won't last, but the payments will. When you go to the mortgage company, ask what amount you are qualified to borrow on a 15-year fixed rate mortgage (no more than a 20-year but try to stay with 15). Look for homes in that range only. If you can't find a home in that range, rent and save money to increase your down payment. As we demonstrated, very little gain or equity is accumulated in the first five years of ownership with a 30-year mortgage, so you're not missing out on anything.

In fact, if I am correct, there will be some great deals coming up very soon. Don't believe the ads where the visibly tense woman picks up the phone and says, "We did?" She then turns to her husband, who has now taken on the posture of great anticipation, and with teary eyes and trembling lips she says, "Honey, we got the loan for the house." What she really should say is, "Honey, don't plan anything for the next 40 years. I just got word that we're in debt up to our eyeballs."

CHAPTER 13

REALITY AND OTHER NUISANCES CREATED BY FACTS

I WANT YOU TO BE HAPPY. To do that, I need to point out some of the self-inflicted things that make us unhappy, so that you won't do those things anymore. That seems a simple enough solution to happiness and, in reality, it is. But then we don't live in a world that is greatly influenced by reality. We live in a world that is *totally* influenced by growth and false promises. And since exponential growth isn't possible, for the good of the cause, maybe we should just continue to ignore reality and go along with the charade that keeps the party from ending early. Just kidding.

We aren't going to ignore reality. Nope, not us — we want to be happy. Paraphrasing something that I said earlier, "If you are truly happy, there is nothing more to gain in life; if you're not happy, you need to get that way."

Abraham Lincoln said, "Most folks are as happy as they make up their minds to be." As strange as it may seem, in truth, we spend very little time considering what makes us unhappy and then using that information to do something about it.

Having the true picture of our current economic situation is critical to making good life decisions that will ensure our long-term goal of happiness. Abraham Lincoln also said, "I am a firm believer in the people. If given the truth, they can be depended upon to meet any national crisis. The great point is to bring them the real facts." Now that's a mouthful.

Honest Abe must not have figured on being a lifelong politician. Trotting out the real facts today would be political suicide. Mr. Lincoln was certainly correct when he stated, the people, if armed with the real facts, could be counted on to meet the crisis. You could count on what the people would do, alright; you could count on them throwing the current politicians out of office in the midst of the panic that would ensue about three minutes after the true facts were announced. The point of this writing is to focus on the true facts as they exist today, so that you don't end up in a panic.

By now, you know all about the growth thing, and hopefully see the impossibility of continuing down that road. Even if it were possible (and it still isn't), it is evident that growth causes a decline in living standards. I remember the first time that a person from a large city told me that they loved living downtown, because they had everything. I thought about that, and agreed. They had pollution, congestion, crime, traffic, and a complete social breakdown from their neighbors — *everything*.

In most instances, growth creates as many problems as it solves. And over the long run, far more disadvantages than benefits. Are cities nicer places to live as they become megalopolises? Are freeways a joyful drive during rush hour? Is getting mugged in broad daylight a thrill that no one should live without? Not in this lifetime or any other. So why do cities just keep getting larger? Is it for the benefit of the citizens, or to keep the growth-oriented economy propped up?

"Normal" living in the United States does require growth. Therefore, we need to elect to be happy rather than to be normal — probably a dumb idea, due to having little or no benefit at all to your Congressperson's or lender's future wealth; but read on and see what you think, after all, charity begins at home.

Let's do a pop quiz. What is the greatest source of conflict between husbands and wives? Go ahead and shout out your answers. I heard football, basketball, baseball, hockey, and the unfair division of housecleaning. No doubt, serious conflict issues, but that isn't what I'm looking for. Aw, there you go: money, cash, currency, moolah, filthy lucre, and long green are the undisputed champions of discord. The title holder of disagreement and the root of most stress and discontent is purely a mistaken perception of having insufficient funds.

I say "mistaken," because no matter how much money humans have, they believe that it isn't enough. There are countless sayings that have survived the decades, such as, "money can't buy you happiness" or "money is the root of all evil" or "money can't buy you love." All are true, but deep down we must not believe them, or we wouldn't spend our short lives banging our heads against the wall trying to acquire more money.

If you really think about it, if money made people happy, rich people would be all but thrilled to death. Of course, they aren't. In fact, statistically, they aren't any happier than poor people. That's because they set out on an impossible mission to find happiness. Possessing money and all the trappings that money can buy really doesn't have anything to do with contentment. Okay, maybe for a couple of weeks, but not long term.

However, not *owing* money can certainly make us happy. Sitting at home on a snowy day reading a book by the fire can be a choice for those with little debt, afforded as a result of financial independence. You may remember that gaining *independence* was the thrust of the Revolutionary War, and high on the list of "things to do today" for our Forefathers.

But for most of Americans, the highest thing on the list of "what to do today" is to go to work, regardless of weather, health, or aspiration, as a result of being one paycheck away from bankruptcy. What fun. Debt and the reasons that we incur debt are often the result of a poorly conceived plan that was meant to create happiness, similar to the ill-conceived plan to make money when you went into that business partnership with your sister-in-law.

So if we know that an endless quest for money is going to cause us to be miserable, why do we constantly borrow money to further our suffering? Even a two year old learns that touching the stove creates undesirable results, but adults seem to have some mental block when it comes to *monetary* pain. Greed, envy, and the perpetual need for growth are the real culprits in this puzzling behavior. But even that does not explain why we don't eventually learn that the stove is hot. I'm not sure that anyone can totally explain why the human race behaves the way it does. But, I do have a theory that I have developed over the years. (I bet that surprises you.)

I believe that what we really want is time, *free time*, to be exact — *Thank God It's Friday*-type free time. The weekends go sailing by at warp speed and vacations compress time like a vacu-matic storage bag. Most of us absolutely love our free time. Yet in our current society, behaving "normally" pretty much eliminates the possibility of having a second cup of coffee.

We have to get to work to pay for the new SUV, the new luxury home, and last year's vacation to Timbuktu, where we paid $500 to ride a camel. The guys in the striped suits aren't the only ones doing time at something they would rather not partake in. Many people do life in an occupation that they nearly detest, for the single purpose of appearing normal. Once you become totally normal, you don't have any free time (remember, you sentenced yourself to a 30-year mortgage and a 60-month car payment). At this point, you no longer have any free time, and you're meaner than a two-headed snake. You're not happy even one little bit. So to be happy, you buy something — *on credit*.

I call it the "bigger boat syndrome." It goes like this. After a week at work of doing exactly what you really didn't want to be doing — combined with the fact that the oldest man in the world just died, fortifying your suspicion that you won't live forever — you make the decision to change your life; you'll buy a boat. The idea here is to buy something that will make you soooo happy on the weekend that the euphoria will propel you through the workweek without having thoughts of strangling anyone.

After the first weekend of rowing, you determine that a motor would *really* make you happy, so you buy one — on credit. After the first weekend with the motor, and during an exceptionally productive rainstorm, you realize that you can get a whole lot further from shore than previously possible with only the oars. You also come to the realization that bailing water while driving the boat over four-foot waves in a torrential downpour has the effect of dampening the pleasure of boating; you are no longer happy.

No problem. You trade in your two-week old boat for a bigger boat with a cabin and an electric bilge pump. This boat includes sleeping quarters designed by Pigmies, which you figure will save on motel bills and make you even happier. (In reality, it would have been cheaper to buy the motel, but you don't know that yet.) After you pay the chiropractic bills, necessitated after sleeping on the new boat, you reevaluate eternal happiness and determine that buying a cabin cruiser with a bathroom and kitchen (a "head" and "galley" for the nautically correct) is the only logical choice. The lake that you keep your new cabin cruiser on is now only slightly longer than the main deck, so you move to your new slip at Marina Del Bankrupt, which is three hours away and a steal at twice the price, according to the marina manager.

By this point in the "bigger boat syndrome," you don't have time to go to the boat any longer, due to the three-hour drive and the recent requirement to work overtime in order to make the combined payment for the boat, slip, insurance, and fuel. At this juncture, you make the decision that any red-blooded American would make: you decide to sell the now used boat.

It is here that you come to realize that *used* boats don't have resale values with a plus sign in front of them. Looking at your loan statement, you realize that your current loan balance *does* have a plus sign in front of it, and seems to be holding its value nicely. The BOAT (which I reminded you earlier stood for **B**reak **O**ut **A**nother **T**housand) is dropping in value faster than Dot Com stock, and has now become a noticeable liability.

The guy at the marina assures you that if you keep the boat for 50 more years, you may be able to sell it as a classic and get some of your money back. That doesn't work out for your immediate plans, due to the fact that you aren't happy and need to sell the boat in order to borrow money for some *new* happiness, in the form of a Harley Davidson similar to Jay Leno's.

Following your divorce, where you were awarded the boat *and* the Harley payment, you tell your friends that you have no idea what went wrong with your marriage. The people who write soap opera scripts don't need imagination, they only need observation. Reality TV has replaced most screenwriters, due to the very real fact that screenwriters couldn't think up anything as bizarre as real life. So what went wrong?

What went wrong is that most people don't believe that there is any way that they can ever have free time, so they try to substitute possessions and perceived social stature to gain happiness. Most children today observe both of their parents working six days per week in a frantic effort to maintain solvency. Most Americans have NO free time. Family and personal relationships have either been cast aside for high-speed careers, or simply because of the additional work time required to service debt and manage the burden of ever-increasing personal possessions. During childhood, our environment and observations shape our beliefs as to what constitutes normal behavior. The above-described lifestyle is unfortunately what most children are geared to perceive as normal, so they repeat the process. And *that* is a very good thing for an economy based on growth and consumption.

This repeated behavior can be witnessed today in a new class of young adults commonly called "boomerang kids." They were raised with little expectation of structured work or contributions to household chores, yet were treated to all of the trappings that their parents' hectic lifestyle could provide. Luxury cars, large homes, the latest electronics, costly entertainment, frequent travel, restaurant meals, and overpriced designer clothes have become *expectations*.

The child heads off to college with a car, cell phone, laptop computer, credit card, tuition, and housing expenses provided by the parents, who continue to incur debt well into the years that they should be investing and saving for retirement. Four years later, hopefully, the parents attend a graduation. After graduation, the kids realize that they can't support themselves in the manner to which they have become accustomed without a lot of hard work and sacrifice. No difficult decision here — they move back home! There are thousands of these kids, and more returning every day. Hmmm, something went wrong with the plan. Luckily, plans can change.

Think *freedom* here. Consider that over the centuries and around the globe, people have risked and given their lives to gain freedom. Freedom from debt is no different. Financial freedom is a wonderful thing. It opens up aspects of your life that you never thought possible. You never thought it was possible, because we have all been programmed for customary behavior, and "customary," in this case, requires debt up to our ears. For most people, financial freedom probably isn't possible, but for you? I have a special deal.

Throughout this book, by using common reason, I have attempted to demonstrate the fact that radical change in the way we live in the good ol' U.S.of A. has no alternative but to take place in the very near future. The pyramid scheme that our economy is based on has run its predictable course. Not so many years ago, if I had told you that the Koreans would be building billion dollar auto plants, you would have thought I was wacky. Today, the Koreans *are* building billion dollar auto plants — in the United States! So have the Japanese. In the meantime, Ford and G.M. are toast.

If I had told you that communist China and poverty-stricken India would be buying the majority of our federal debt, while at the same time becoming some of our largest trading partners, you would have thought that I had gotten into some brown bottle medicine too early in the day. What if you had been told down at the coffee shop in the year 2000 that the *medium* new home price would hit $238,000 in late 2005 and continue to climb through 2006? The home isn't worth *more*, your money is worth *less*. But, according to reliable Government Math accountants, we don't have core inflation.

What if just a few years ago it had been suggested that small business in America would be on the ropes, due to Wal-Mart's Chinese imports? Had I told you that nearly all of our major air carriers would be in bankruptcy by 2005, it would have been laughable. Announcements (in a three month period) that more than 150,000 Americans are losing their high-paying jobs at Ford, G.M., AT&T, Kraft, Delphi, Dana, Whirlpool, etc., don't even make the front page! Once-bankrupt K-Mart purchasing a beleaguered Sears, or how about $23 billion in mergers taking place in a one-week period as U.S. companies struggle for survival and cut their work forces? If you can look at all these pesky *facts* and believe that everything is okey-dokey, have your doctor check your medicine.

The need for perpetual growth has created a society of debtors, and exponential growth has run its course. Change is coming, and for the unprepared it won't be pretty. The rich, in truth, are going to get richer, and the American middle class, as we know it, will vanish. Mathematically, and in this global setting, there is just no other way.

Just for the sake of argument, let's say that I am dead wrong about the impossibility of exponential growth. At the same time, pretend that the Chinese government begins to feel sorry for America's middle class and raises the Chinese workers wages to $20.00 per hour in a caring gesture in an effort to level the playing field. And, while we are playing pretend, let's also say that they require 25% of all the Chinese people to drive American-made autos. While we are visiting la-la-land, shall we also make believe that the Chinese and other Asians won't remember that the United States, for many years, excluded them from immigration status and even denied citizenship to those already living here? The point is that it really doesn't matter: adhering to the concept of living with low debt and greater personal freedom shouldn't have to be forced on us; it's a formula for a better life in any economy.

In business, the term "risk management" is used every day. It simply means that any new venture or large business expenditure needs to be analyzed to determine what the worst case scenario may be should things not work out exactly as planned. We need to practice risk management in everyday life. When you decide to go down and sign that 30-year mortgage or that 60-month auto loan, run some numbers to determine the risk involved. The lottery is a far better bet. You may lose your money, but you won't commit your entire working life to doing so.

Risk management in our personal lives should certainly include finances, but, more importantly, should include time. You may earn more money, but you can't earn more time.

I would like for you to do something for me. If at all possible, take some time for yourself. Think about what financial freedom, and the resulting free time, would be like. Take a mini-trip, even if it is to a motel or cottage 50 miles from home. Get away from the phone and all of the distractions of everyday life. Dedicate the time away for the single purpose of considering your life as it exists on that leisurely day, and then consider what it would be like if you could spend a significant portion of your remaining time doing the things that you enjoy most. If you have manageable debt, you can take the time to do the things that make life fun and happy. If you don't, well — Hi-Ho, Hi-Ho, it's off to work you go.

Give some thought to how you feel about your work. If you find yourself living for the weekends and constantly wishing it were Friday, don't you believe that something is terribly wrong? Why would you want to spend the rest of your life wishing it were over? That's what wishing for Friday represents. So why can't you make a change? Let me guess — you have bills to pay, right? Someone held you down and made you sign all of those debt instruments against your will. The next time that you wish it were Friday, consider what I have just said. You voluntarily traded your life for debt; otherwise, you wouldn't be wishing it away.

It isn't easy to comprehend what free time would be like for the average American, because you've had very little. Most of your life has prepared you to buy everything that was within your reach and pledge your entire life to pay for it. Couple that with the necessity of ever-increasing production and its associated stress, and you have life in America's fast lane. A society that is totally predicated on growth for its existence has no alternative but to encourage that behavior. That's why Americans are the Consumer Olympic gold, silver, bronze, and pot metal champions. You, however, don't have to participate.

The initial time that you spend contemplating what it would be like to have free time will be difficult. You can't change a lifetime of habits in one long weekend. Clearing the clutter out of your brain that exists from daily demands won't be accomplished overnight. Set aside a little time each day to plan a better lifestyle. Once you get even a glimpse of financial freedom, you'll never go back. We must remember that not so long ago, life was much simpler in the United States and it can be again for those who choose to pursue that end.

If you do choose to live simply and live well, you may find yourself neighbors to the rich and famous. Yep, the rich and famous are scouring America for old-fashioned little communities where they can hang out. They are searching for what they have determined that money can't buy: peace and quiet. You may already have what the rich and famous want. There is more than a little irony there, for sure.

CHAPTER 14

LIVE SIMPLE, LIVE WELL

SO HERE YOU ARE AT THE CROSSROADS, trying to decide whether to believe "The Biggest Lie Ever Believed," or whether to believe ol' Mike and make a few changes around the home place. The honest truth is, I don't want you to believe me. I want you to think about all of the things that we have discussed. I want you to verify, check, and double check everything that I have said. Then I want you to make decisions using your new-found or re-found knowledge to do what is best *for you.*

America is still a relatively free place to live, and that is about as good as it gets. You are free to make choices that will affect the rest of your life. You are free to change work today, should you wish to. You are free to get in your car tomorrow and move to another state. Just be careful that your freedom to make choices doesn't cause you to make choices that take away your freedom.

Earlier, I included one of my back porch analogies: "If you find that you're on the wrong train, get off at the next stop. It makes getting back home a much shorter trip." Take a hard look at your personal financial situation. Are you on the right train? If you have huge car payments, super-sized house payments, and a credit card statement that rivals the national debt of Guatemala, you're probably bound for a financial destination that is not conducive to snowballs. If you have boarded the "debt express," get off the train — *now.* If you don't currently have huge debt, it will be a much shorter trip to where we are going. And remember: there's hope for anyone who has the desire to experience financial freedom.

Getting started toward a simpler (and better) life is fraught with obstacles placed there by tradition and convention. It will be necessary to break from tradition and convention should you wish to simplify your life, and that isn't easy. Sometimes it helps to gaze at that person in the mirror while considering who it is that you are really trying to please. I'll give you a hint, it's not the neighbors. Tradition, peer pressure, and ego — or whatever else it is that makes us do dumb stuff — are not easy to explain.

Consider that in the 1970s, someone, somewhere, apparently made the decision that bell-bottom pants and orange furniture were in style. Hairstyles looked like something out of a horror movie and the new car designs appeared to be fitting transportation for the starring monsters. Who said that these styles were cool? I'm sure it was some poor deranged designer recently released from a place where they should have been required to stay, but all the same, the public went along with it.

Why? Because everyone else was doing it. Having an orange car, orange furniture, and orange shag carpet was normal, yet if you possessed those things today, you would be labeled as some kind of kook. This "being normal" thing is a problem and if you continue to practice it, you will most certainly join a very large group of burned-out and bankrupt U.S. citizens who maintain the same beliefs. You won't be lonely. Broke, yes, but not lonely.

Nutty group behavior is a subject well beyond my expertise. I remain an astonished side-line observer in that category. Selling the masses on wacky ideas that offer little benefit to anyone other than the sellers, continues to be a national pastime and has become acceptable as standard commerce. Don't tell me you weren't tempted to buy a pet rock. While not making light of the subject, Jim Jones convinced more than 900 semi-normal American followers into going to Guyana with him and jointly committing suicide by drinking poisoned Kool-Aid™! Selling the idea that spending the majority of your life paying for overpriced cars and houses isn't much of a challenge in comparison.

For those who secretly believe that growth will save the day, the suggestions that follow will not be easy to swallow. But then if you thought growth of that magnitude was remotely possible, you would have run the book page by page through the garbage disposal, or a shredder, after chapter two.

The information and advice that I have provided thus far was meant for all ages. For the younger people, getting a grip on reality, and living well in spite of it, was my goal. For the middle-aged group, a plan to correct past errors and change course for a happier and better life are my wishes. For the older group, I hope to give you some new ideas to prepare for a better retirement.

While I will separate the final plans for each group, I do wish that (even if it doesn't affect you personally) you will read each one. Hopefully, you can help someone else to financial freedom and a sustainable lifestyle, or at least provide them with pertinent and truthful information so that they can make educated choices.

I'm going to start with the oldest group first, not because age has its privileges, but because they have the least time to dally around!

THE NEAR-RETIREMENT AGE: What is the age for retirement, anyway? If I asked that question on the street, I'd find that 95% of respondents would answer either 62 or 65. That would make 95% of the population wrong. Indentured servitude was banned long ago. The age for retirement is the age at which one can *afford* to retire. I often hear the comment, "Oh, you're too young to retire." Let me decipher that statement for you, "You're too young to retire, because I'm much older, and I couldn't consider retirement under my debt load." Misery loves company.

The reason that 95% of people would answer 62 or 65 is because they are practicing convention. This is good, because 100% of our lenders and government leaders are counting on that type of behavior. Most people *do* retire after age 62, because they didn't plan to retire sooner. How does one retire prior to the prescribed golden years? One word — planning. A person must have a greater desire and passion for leisure time and simple pleasures than that for portraying false wealth by incurring debt. Repeating an earlier statement, "Never get mad at a person because they are smarter than you; it isn't their fault."

We all need a plan. If you don't know where you are going, any airplane will do. I may as well start with the toughest subject first, and that would be personal housing. Although housing deals with the highest single cost that most people will ever incur, it is, at the same time, about as touchy to approach as a pet porcupine.

We're messing with tradition, emotion, and convention that rival mom and apple pie. But we gotta talk about it, because that same cherished possession that you call "home" has the very real ability to rob you of much of your life. Not your working life — your leisure life, and your retirement. Should you continue to practice convention, your working life is as secure as Fort Knox.

If you are approaching retirement or if you would like to consider a plan for an early retirement, determine what influence your present home is going to have on those plans. Housing cannot and will not continue to increase at the current maniacal pace. It is just not a logical or mathematical possibility. There will be a significant decline in home prices, and the effects will be far reaching. Interest rates will increase and prices will go down. Affordability for larger homes will be out of reach for the average person. The perfect financial storm is brewing from years of inflation and socially induced illogical housing choices. The end result will take its toll on the wealth that you *believe* you have accumulated in personal housing.

So, if your plans for retirement include selling your present home in order to cash in on the equity, do it NOW. Even if you have a few years before you had planned to sell, inconvenience yourself a little now and clip the coupon. Sure, the prices may go up slightly longer, but if the market turns at your age, you will never weather the storm waiting for prices to return. Practice "risk management." *The best time to sell at a profit is when you have a buyer that offers you one.*

In most cases, if you have lived in your present home for 24 months or more, there are no Federal capital gains taxes due on the sale of your primary residence. Singles who qualify can exclude $250,000 in capital gains tax, and qualifying married couples filing jointly can exclude $500,000 in gains. If you are going to make more than the allowed tax exempt gain, and you meet the 24 month rule, the taxable portion is a long-term capital gain, and will be taxed at a flat rate. Tax questions and the final outcome for your personal situation should be asked of your accountant or tax counsel prior to selling.

Far too great a portion of Americans' personal wealth has been funneled into the belief that a home is an investment. Yet a home is an investment that has no physical monetary return unless sold. It is an investment that costs you an inordinate percentage of your lifetime net income. A home is an investment that robs a great deal of your lifetime capital from being put to work in real investments that would have created a residual income for your retirement. A home provides shelter, and if you can once get past the negative psychological barriers that are associated with the thought of scaling down, your home can still become an investment. Don't wait until you believe the market has peaked; convert your home equity into an investment on your own terms.

Reflect on ways that you could logically scale down. Consider the portions of your home that you use on a daily basis. Think about the ways in which you use that space and how you see using space in retirement. Be realistic: at retirement age, you have probably enjoyed cleaning and maintaining about as much as you ever care to. Consider how you could condense your living space, and at the same time be comfortable. Don't set out for image, it won't get you where you want to go.

Want to feel better about your decision to scale down and take an earlier retirement? Ask your friends who questioned your sanity when you told them your plans for scaling back, and who are the same friends that recently refinanced their McMansion for the third time in three years, to join you on Wednesday and Thursday for an overnight trip to the mountains. When they say, "Are you kidding, we both have to go to work." You then say, "Oh, gee, that's right. We must have forgotten." Nah-na nah-na nah-na.

Another tactical mistake that is often voluntarily committed is working for the majority of one's lifetime with the idea of rewarding yourself in the future. It's interesting that so many people know exactly what their future has in store. They *must* know, or otherwise they wouldn't plan for events that will take place 30 years from now.

I have observed countless people who hold onto dreams throughout their working lives only to see those dreams fade away as time passes. They have dreamt about a big home or a small farm or a large workshop all of their lives. So when they retire, they plow all of their money into those things that they had hoped would make them happy, only to find that their interests and abilities have changed with age. The dreams have now become possessions that are a tremendous burden both from a financial and maintenance standpoint. Think about what you *really* want to do. Chances are if you *really* wanted to do something bad enough, you would already have done it. At least you should have.

I remember the place and time that I first realized the fallacy of putting off the things that I truly wanted to enjoy until after standard old-age retirement. A friend and I were walking into a restaurant in Delta Junction, Alaska, one early summer day, when a tour bus pulled in across the parking lot. The bus had to park well away from the building, which created perhaps a 150-foot walk to the door.

As the occupants began filing out of the bus, I realized they were retired folks on their dream vacation to Alaska. Some were using canes, some even walkers, and the large gravel on the parking lot was nearly impossible for them to negotiate. As they slowly struggled across the lot, I thought, *what a shame. All of those years spent working with the self-promise for future reward, and this is it*? I made a decision then and there to never base my future on false promises, as those folks had. And I never have. Less than 30 days later, I quit a very desirable and high-paying job as a tech with RCA Alaska Communications to attend auctioneers school. I had always wanted to be an auctioneer. Was I sorry in the end? Not one little bit.

It's all about debt, and the daily pressure to appear monetarily successful in the eyes of our peers, that is the great robber baron of our freedom. Acquiring money and the trappings of expensive personal property doesn't signify a good life. There are no U-Hauls going to the cemetery. The desire to buy happiness with long-term debt, along with extended planning into the golden years for obtaining your just reward, will rob you of your life, just like those folks on that tour bus, all of those years ago.

If it takes selling your home and scaling down, or selling the new car and buying a bargain, or even relocating to an area where the cost of living allows you to have financial freedom — do it! You'll *never* be sorry. An old fellow in Seattle once told me, "Keep on doing what you're doing, son. No man has ever laid on his death bed and said, 'I wish I'd spent more time at work.'" That old fellow knew of what he spoke. Don't just go hog-wild and get crazy on me with this idea. Plan it out. Have some fun in life — it's a short trip.

If you are at an age that doing everything that has been suggested thus far won't do the trick, you may not be able to *completely* retire. But semi-retirement isn't half bad, particularly if you can accomplish some form of retirement, several years ahead of schedule.

I know that you have heard someone mention semi-retirement a hundred times. But talking and doing are two very different actions. Semi-retirement for those wishing to practice it today has never been more feasible. There is a qualified work force shortage that won't wait a minute. The sage knowledge and stability that older workers bring to any organization is extremely valuable. The employers don't wish to see most of those workers leave and are willing to make a deal.

I can't possibly cover every job category or position, so I will give you examples that could be molded into most situations. I have a friend who took early retirement and who has helped me in my business for years now. The catch — don't ask him to do that on the weeks that he and his wife are traveling. The benefit for me is that I get an honest, trustworthy individual who is rested and energized during the times that I need help. I also get a person who has a broad knowledge from a lifetime of experience. My friend gets the additional income that he desires for extra fun money, and to subsidize his retirement. We both win.

So, what if I needed him during the times that he is on vacation (which is a lot of the time)? I have another friend who practices the same thing and who has chosen the same means to early retirement. When one is away, the other fills in. This arrangement can be set up on a permanent basis for a person that desires structure. One employee works for a given period of time (for instance, a month), the other employee then works the following month, and they continue to alternate. The employer really doesn't mind, so long as he or she has qualified help. In many instances, this rotation is superior to having only one person, due to revitalized energy levels and the benefit of the old axiom, "Two heads are better than one."

I have yet another friend who took early retirement and eventually wanted to do something part time. He and one of his retired cronies overheard a man complaining in the coffee shop that he couldn't get painters to complete the exterior painting of his new house. Long story short, on a lark, these two guys offered to paint the house. They did a great job and made excellent money. Word spread, and today they pick and choose *what* they want to paint, *when* they want to paint, *if* they want to paint, and spend the rest of their time enjoying retirement. That works.

I like to use real examples, as the two above demonstrate. Another acquaintance was offered early retirement, and while he really didn't need additional money, he wanted to remain active. He decided that he would try e-bay. Without going into detail (there are books on the subject), his e-bay business became so successful that he could easily live on that income alone. Far more important, he was having an absolute blast doing it. He described it as being on a giant treasure hunt and finding a few diamonds in the rough every day. Many people perform better in second careers, due to choosing something that they *truly* enjoy. Now, *there's* a concept! I can go on and on citing real examples of people who have conquered the beast, but you get the gist of how it's done.

Where do you want to retire? This is a subject that could be so lengthy that we could talk about it until the cows come home. Relax, I wouldn't do that to you. Actually, I would, but I know you want to get to the bottom line, so I'll just hit the high points. This is an area of consideration that could cause, shall we say, some discourse among married partners. I'm going to recommend that you move, even if you don't want to scale down. I heard the groans. I even heard someone say, "WELL, the nerve of this nincompoop, telling us where to live. I swear, I've never seen the likes." Don't get your backs up until you've heard me out.

If you retire on, say, Friday, and stay in the same place that you have lived for years, what will happen on Monday? The answer is that *you* won't go to work; same goes for Tuesday and the rest of the week. The neighbors, your friends, and your children *will* go to work on Monday and Tuesday and the rest of the week. You know why? They didn't retire and they have debt. In the meantime, you realize that watching daytime TV and reading the paper is not providing quite the level of enjoyment that you had so long anticipated.

The only thing that changed is that you aren't going to work, which leaves about 60 hours per week to fill with something that up until now was not a problem. You may even get so disheartened that you stop back by your old workplace to ask whether the person who replaced you (even though you were irreplaceable) needs any advice. The new person tells you that they really don't need any help — there really hadn't been all that much to learn. Now totally depressed, you head back to the house because it's 2 PM and *Days of Our Lives* is coming on. You like that show, because those people are in perpetual, dreadful situations and have worse problems than you do.

What we have here is a very, very common case of incompatibility. You see, 30-plus years of going to work created somewhat of a routine that is often referred to as a "rut." I believe that one of the greatest oversights that the majority of retirees make is the failure to *plan* a life-changing shift in daily activities, as they move into retirement.

Far too many retirees report that retirement is not satisfying. I believe that those people simply failed to plan for changes that could have made retirement the most enjoyable part of their entire lives. Failure to change your lifestyle, and hanging around in the same house with the same surroundings in the same mode that you have practiced for the last 30 years, could easily resemble last season's reruns for the foreseeable future.

The life that you have lived up to now may not have required significant planning, other than that of setting the alarm clock and going to work. You have now entered a new period of freedom, and change you must, unless you really do enjoy the paper and daytime soaps.

I'll give you three guesses as to who is in charge of making those necessary changes, and the first two don't count. I'm also going to gamble that these adjustments in your life really shouldn't include a larger home, bigger lawn, more maintenance, and greater stress. Once you get the hang of this thing, the thought of "scaling down" can get downright exciting.

Retirees enjoy being in a community and living around others who share their likes and dislikes. For that matter, we all do. But retirees have more options in that regard. Having neighbors and friends that are in the same mode creates a very low-stress and enjoyable lifestyle. A case in point that helps to demonstrate the undesirable results of mixing people in *different* modes can clearly be seen on our highways. Some people wear seat belts and drive the speed limit, while others choose to drive 80 MPH without seat belts while reading the paper and talking on their cell phones. The product of these differences is stress, accidents, and death on a daily basis. So what if everyone was to obey the speed limit, devote 100% of their attention to driving, and wore their seat belts? The result would be low stress and far fewer accidents and deaths. So, why don't we choose the latter? Because drivers are in different age groups, have different values, and operate in different modes. The outcome is conflict.

Ah, yes — conflict, defined as "emotional disturbance," and we didn't like emotional disturbance *before* we retired. Therefore, we should plan not to participate in voluntary, emotional disturbance *after* we retire (as in 30 years is enough). You see, conflict is avoidable for the most part by hanging around in an area where the other people share the same interests that you do. Those with compatible circumstances make better neighbors and companions for activities. Their plans are similar to yours; they didn't go to work today, and they aren't planning any such goings-on in the future.

Having neighbors that play loud rap music until 2 AM — or the people who bought the house next door who raise pit bulls, which prefer your yard for relieving themselves and your cat as opposed to Alpo — is not conducive to a conflict-free retirement. But retirees encounter these types of situations every day. Why? *They thought retirement was going to come to them, rather than them going to retirement.* Not a chance. Nope, just figure things are going to remain pretty much the same around the old hacienda until such time as *you* make a change.

I can't emphasize enough the importance that I place on having people with the same interests and lifestyles for creating a happy and desirable community. I believe that this may be the single most important piece of information that I personally have ever linked to general happiness. Move to an area where the majority of the residents enjoy doing what you enjoy doing. Where most of the other residents are free to come and go as they please.

I watched my own parents practice this for 30+ years. They would leave home every spring and stay the entire summer in a mobile home that they owned in a lake community. They had accomplished this by moving to a smaller, less expensive "lock and leave" type winter home early in retirement. The other residents of their little lake community were, by and large, on the same page. They all enjoyed one another's company, whether cooking on the grill, cruising around the lake on a pontoon boat, playing cards, having morning coffee on the deck, or just plain kicking back. My parents would stay until winter freeze-up and were back at spring break-up. Life was good for 31 years of retirement in this simple community that provided nothing more than compatibility. But then, that's a lot.

Still not convinced, huh? I still haven't changed my mind about your selling that big house and moving, but for all you Doubting Thomases, there is a way to test the waters before you commit to selling the house. Recreational Vehicles (RVs) have given people the chance to sample a retirement lifestyle, without betting the farm.

Buy a *good used* RV, or rent a place in a retirement community that fits your clothes. You know, where the people are acting like you do (God forbid). Try it for a season. If you don't like it, move back home and nothing terrible was risked (except that your house may have gone down in value). You can sell the RV, and with very little monetary loss, you had a trial run at a new life of leisure. I'll give you a little warning, though. I've sold countless large homes for people who have tried the above experiment, and *none* of them are back. You see, they didn't like conflict.

I could go on and on about ways to retire or semi-retire, but it wouldn't help. The burning desire to be financially free and to get up every morning asking yourself, "What would I like to do today?" rather than "What do I *have* to do today?" comes from within. I can only hope that I have given you the inspiration to try it. Trust me on one thing: there is much to gain and little to lose, and that is risk management at its finest.

We need to move on to the people in the middle-aged group: those who have ten or more years of work remaining.

CHAPTER 15

TO THE MIDDLE AGED: CHANGE COURSE— NOW!

WHILE I AM DEVOTING THIS CHAPTER to those who are in the middle of the pack, so to speak, all of the information in the last chapter should be taken into consideration due to the very real fact that even with Miracle Cream, you're getting older by the day. The main difference between your group and the near-retirees is that in the next ten years, many of the serious issues that we have discussed throughout this book will have come to pass. No crystal ball is necessary for that news.

I often use an analogy from my flying days to demonstrate the necessary urgency for a radical change in course. In the technical language of the bush pilot, this can be better stated as, "You better do something quick, or you're going to get a once in a lifetime opportunity to practice a controlled crash-landing in real time." This situation can occur when a pilot suddenly realizes that an unanticipated cross wind has caused him to drift well off course in the direction of a place called "nowhere." Failure to make an immediate and radical course correction will result in the fuel reaching empty prior to the plane reaching the airport. This is not an acceptable plan for the insurance company.

Making minor corrections at this point would only allow the plane to crash nearer to the airport. If the pilot is going to make the landing field safely, a radical correction, and then staying on course, is mandatory. The same goes for life. Take a bearing on where you are going and estimate how much fuel you have left in your tank to get there. If it appears you are running dangerously short, change course.

Age can be substituted for fuel in the above example. You may run out of life before you get where you want to go, and that can't be good. The prospect of working until you die for the single purpose of making ends meet kind of rains on your parade, doesn't it?

Countless millions of baby boomers will have taken retirement by 2016. Medicare will be at, or near, the point of insolvency, and Social Security will be circling the drain. Not only will these boomers be taking moolah out of the system, but they won't be putting any back in. At least the ones who take my advice in the last chapter won't be. They will be retired, and their most stressful decision will be what to barbeque for dinner. Ah, yes — the good life is possible, if you can keep your head in the game after the half-time show.

When I say the boomers won't be putting anything back in, I'm not *just* talking about Social Security and Medicare payments. If they have planned at all, they won't need most of the costly things that were necessary during their former child-rearing and working years. Furniture, cars, homes, computers, electronics — already got 'em, and don't want anymore.

Retirees for the most part are just not big consumers of the aforementioned items. Once more: how old are retirees? Hey, you're getting the hang of this thing. Retirees are as old as they planned to be. Some are 35, some are 85, and some never are. It's important that we take a moment to understand that retirement is not necessarily synonymous with age and the old folk's home. In fact, rather than continue to refer to our group as retirees, how about we just call them "permanent vacationers," or PVs. The word *vacation* is defined in *Webster's* as "A period of rest from work." That's much better than the word *retire*, which is defined as "to withdraw from use." So that's it, then — we're going to be PVs from here on out.

It's said that America's future is in electronics and information. This is the dazzling electronic generation. Let me hear a big BOO-YAH for all the wonderful innovations that have made our lives so much easier. It just brings tears to my eyes to imagine that through recent advances in technology, it is now possible to work 24-7. How fantastic for mankind. The advent of cell phones has made it possible to hate your job from the privacy of your own bathroom.

Not so many years ago, it would have been impossible for your boss or your customers to reach you any place on earth 24-7. But with today's socially advanced technology, you can flip open your cell phone and whip out your laptop while driving your 300 horsepower SUV at 3 MPH in rush hour traffic and conduct business between bites of your Big Mac. Run up Old Glory and play the National Anthem. How could life get better than that? Could someone please call 911? We have a mental emergency — we're nuts!

If you can see where most PVs (age 35 or 85) are going to look forward to holding onto this nutty behavior right into their permanent vacation, you can also see where they are going to look forward to ingrown toenails and root canals. I bet you didn't know that most PVs don't even like electronics. Well, they don't, because they're complicated. They have seen their lives become ever increasingly complex and have enjoyed all of it that they can stand. Take phones for instance.

Most baby boomers remember when phones were simple. All they wanted to do was talk to someone and then hang up. The instructions for a phone went like this: "Pick up the receiver (the thing on top that looks like a dog bone), listen to see if it is buzzing; if not, reverse the ends and listen again. Now, determine what number you would like to dial by locating it in the telephone book, which is conveniently printed on paper in alphabetical order. Push the buttons on your telephone that have corresponding numbers to those printed in the telephone book. When you are finished talking, put the dog bone back down where you got it." That's it, the total operating instructions.

My cell phone has a manual the size of the *Reader's Digest*. "But," you say, "this retiring generation will be different." Oh, sure they will. I'm confident that they will flock to the electronic stores in droves, if only to purchase the newest, most complicated electronic device known to man for the single purpose of assuring themselves that being a PV allows them to never so much as crack the manual. Ha!

Remember what happens when there aren't enough shoppers? Yes, that's right, whoever is in the White House, soon won't be. While PVs *won't* consume all the things that keeps America humming along, they *will* be major league consumers of the gas that keeps the economic engine running — as in Social Security, Medicare, and discounted National Parks passes. You might say business, as we know it, is taking a turn for the worse. But then, that's what we've been talking about since Chapter 1.

Government and Big Business have known for years that the boomers would upset the proverbial apple cart. Count on it. They have also known that anyone who tried to do anything about it could count on extended unemployment. That creates the basis for an easy decision — lie like a rug.

Preparing to live comfortably in this new environment and, at the same time, enjoying your life everyday will require a more significant departure from normal behavior as compared to those in the near-retirement group. In some ways, you people in the middle are in better shape for making the necessary adjustments, due to having more time for doing so.

I have previously said about as much as I can about housing and automobiles. Over their working life, the *average* person could retire *unassisted* from the savings and the consequential long-term investment proceeds of practicing restraint in the areas of transportation and shelter alone. Consider that last statement — it's huge. The answer for most people to live a better life with the real possibility of becoming an early Permanent Vacationer lies in making better lifelong choices on housing and vehicles. Vehicles are transportation and homes are shelter. The complete understanding of those principals alone spells retirement with a capital R. Can't say it enough times: "Live simple, live well."

I think I heard someone way in the back say, "It's easy for you to say plan to be a PV early, but we flatly don't have any extra money as it is." I can respond to that statement best by telling you a story about an actual experience that I had years ago. I was attending a seminar in Seattle, and the lecturer was asking each of us to put back a little money each month in a tax-deferred retirement fund. One of the attendees stopped him and said that he didn't have any extra money to contribute. The lecturer asked the gentleman if he made more than minimum wage. He responded curtly, "Of course I do." The lecturer asked if he knew anyone who made minimum wage. He responded, "Yes, I do." The lecturer now asked if the person making minimum wage were alive or dead. The puzzled gentleman replied, "Alive, of course." The lecturer, with stern conviction, replied, "Then you *could* have extra money to put into retirement, you just don't want to make the effort, and therefore I can't help you." Whoa. It got real quiet in that big room.

That statement had a profound effect, not only on the gentleman who had asked the question, but on everyone in the room. The man who asked the question, while temporarily embarrassed, remained in the seminar for every minute of the next two days. He had learned an important truth about himself. Whacking a person over the head with the truth is not grounds for abuse. It could, however, be grounds for some free time called "retirement," or in our case, permanent vacation.

Scaling down for most red-blooded American capitalists is viewed as a visible sign of failure. Since we tend to wear our wealth on our sleeves by openly displaying high-profile personal possessions, selling the same and scaling back surely must be a sign of financial difficulty. God forbid it could have anything to do with deductive reasoning, such as considering that your house payment will last slightly longer than you will.

At the very least, we are concerned about what our peers will think when they see us scaling back. Living in the smaller (but sensible) home, buying that two- or three-year-old car, and taking a more affordable vacation in lieu of a $10,000 cruise may all appear as visible signs of failure. In actuality, they may be the pinnacle of realization, success, and self-assurance. It takes self-confidence to be abnormal.

As humans, we want to fit in and be perceived as being typical. The problem is, that in the very near future, being typical could very well mean being broke. Misery truly does love company. I know that, because when I try to convince people that they are on a downhill grade without brakes, they say, "I'll have a lot of company if what you say is true." And *that* makes you feel better! That would be like saying, "I hear they are going to hang you today," and you cheerfully say, "Yeah, but they're hanging a bunch of other people, too, so I don't feel so bad."

Those in the middle not only face changing their own ways, but must still consider their children. One of the patent excuses that "typical" people use for justifying debt and working their lives away is, "We want to leave something for our kids." There is something to be said for that reasoning. Most people who work longer have more debt and stress and tend to die earlier, and, therefore, the kids will have their house before they get too old to enjoy it. Good plan.

If you really, really mean that you would like to leave your kids something, you need the advice of a professional child-rearing psychologist. In order to accomplish that, I need to make an adjustment. Where the heck is that other hat? Oh, here it is. Okay, ol' Doc Mike will see you now. What were we talking about? Oh yeah, you wanted to leave your kids something so you figured on working yourself to death at an early age so you wouldn't be a burden to them and they could have your car. I have a better idea.

Slow your life down. Spend more time with your kids and grandkids *now*. Dead people are poor conversationalists and you ain't gonna live forever; actually, if you keep working ten-hour days and stressing out over the McMansion and new SUV payment, it may *seem* like forever. The greatest gift that you can leave your kids is to teach them the values and virtues of family, friends, and a good and simple lifestyle that doesn't include a $10,000 credit card balance. Spend the time, even with your older kids, helping them to understand the pointless insanity of the apparent belief that the person who dies with the largest mortgage and most angles on their roof, wins.

There is a catch. You have to practice what you preach. Ouch! Show them by example that you are willing to change your own lives in order to extract more of the real essence that is there for the taking. Help them to understand that our world is changing, but that it doesn't mean that life is over. It's just the beginning for those who can shed debt and peer pressure. I truly believe that life will be better for those individuals who can make these adjustments than it was for their parents. Work, my friends, is overrated. *These* are the things that you can leave your kids, not a blueprint for working like a dog and incurring debt until it's too late to even get a sniff of the roses. Smelling roses from the root side isn't what I had in mind.

"But what about college costs? How are we going to pay for our kid's college without working until we are 106?" That's easy — don't. Whew! That stirred up a bee's nest, didn't it? I still have my psychologist hat on, so I'll give you Doc Mike's slant on paying for college.

I mentioned earlier that many of today's parents feel the obligation to raise their children until they turn age 55 or until they (the parents) are personally dead or bankrupt. Have you ever seen the bumper sticker on the back of a motor home that says, "We're spending our kids inheritance"? Most kids would say, good, you worked all your life and deserve it. For the ones who question your having an enjoyable retirement at their expense, something went wrong in the child-rearing experience. Probably the promise to pay all of their college costs.

It's called reward without work, or reward without risk. Practicing this activity from birth to age 22 can simulate, to the untrained eye, normality. Take the example of having a child who jumped up and down on the couch until age six. At age six and one day, you determine that not only is this practice annoying, but the couch is now only six inches high. So you scream, "Quit jumping on the couch," and send him to his room, telling him not to come out until he is seven. This is a little confusing to the child, who up to now had no clue that jumping on the couch was a no-no. Stay with me here.

Due to wanting your child to live better than you, you promise to love, cherish, and obey them when they ask for money, cell phones, cars, computers, their own bathroom, and college costs. You live up to your promise and pay for all of these wonderful things. At age 22, and just after college graduation, you expect that your child will now obtain gainful employment. This is a little confusing to the child (big child by now) who, up to that point, had no clue that the money that you were using to pay for all these ongoing costs was associated with work. Worse yet, they weren't associating the college degree with them *personally* entering the workforce. The shock of realizing, at age 22, that they are responsible for their own lives, causes them to ask, "So, how are you fixed for paying for my graduate school?"

How do we deal with college costs? We actually ask the kids to help pay for their own education by working. You see, doing so can help kids grasp the concept that a college education leads to employment. "Oh, my GOD! The next thing you know, you will be suggesting that they buy their own car!" Yes, I will, and a cheap one at that.

Our three sons actually still talk to us after being brutally raised under the hostile conditions mentioned above. It appears that they may even like us. Each took a different path in life that fit their very different personalities.

The oldest son was an excellent student and began college on an academic scholarship. He worked at McDonald's to assist with his college costs and completed two years. After the second year, and by his own decision, he chose not to continue. He wanted something different from life. Today, he has given us four wonderful grandchildren, has good and stable employment, and lives simply and happily in a lifestyle which *he* has chosen. He and his wife own their own *home* and practice a lifestyle that is both affordable and enjoyable. They spend much of their free time with friends and family doing the things that *they* want to do. Time to camp and coach kids' ball. Time to plant a garden and go hunting: Time to live! Life doesn't offer us more than that.

Our middle son spent time in the employ of the U.S. Navy and attended college on the G.I. Bill, while working part-time at an assisted living center to make ends meet. Once the G.I. Bill was extinguished, he worked for a company who paid for a portion of his continued education so long as he remained in their employment. He attended school during the evenings and weekends, and received a degree from a prominent business school. Why did he work so hard and put in such long hours at night and on weekends to achieve a degree without assistance from his mother and me? He wanted to.

Why didn't he take out huge student loans rather than suffer through the rigors of working to put himself through school? He had aced eighth grade math and figured out that he wasn't going to live long enough to pay the loans back, while at the same time eating regularly. You see, lots of kids go to college, not because they really want to, but because their parents are paying for it. And given the choice, it beats the heck out of working. Our middle son now independently owns a successful corporate training company. What did his mother and I give him? The personal strength, wisdom, support, and business guidance to allow him to do just that.

That brings us to our youngest son, who had no interest in attending college. After high school, I arranged for him to go to work for one of my friends in Alaska, on a hay farm, no less. This was a learning experience that no college could have provided. Sometimes knowing what you don't want to do is more important than knowing what you do want to do. When he returned to Colorado, he became employed in the electrical trade. At age 22, I convinced him to save and buy a home, rather than a new truck.

Today, his home is affordable, his vehicles are paid for, and his work pays the equivalent of what most of his college grad counterparts are making. He spends his free time doing what he loves — hunting, fishing, camping, and traipsing around the Rocky Mountains. He can spend his ample free time doing all of the things that are his passion due to his financial freedom. His mother and I gave him, not money, but knowledge and the understanding of what really is important in life. Oh, yes — we also practiced what we preached. It didn't hurt that bad.

So, when I hear that college is unaffordable for kids whose parents can't afford to send them, or that success isn't possible without a college education, I just smile and remain thankful that our kids didn't know that.

I have covered transportation, housing, and now college educations. I have no intention of telling you how to raise your kids: the examples are simply real events, and the opinions of the outcomes are simply those of ol' Doc Mike. As humans, we are most proud of what we accomplish by our own efforts. I do believe that many kids are robbed of becoming their own person, by nothing more than the good intentions of their parents attempting to make life easier for them. The problem is that life isn't easy for the unprepared or inexperienced.

In this day of two-person incomes and harried schedules, eating out has become commonplace. Let's face it, no one should be expected to work all day and then become responsible for "what's for dinner." Continually asking that question of a tired and underappreciated working spouse could result in the need for medical attention. The alternative to being clobbered with a frying pan has become eating out. This alternative is way expensive.

Eating out is one of those items that has been flogged unmercifully by inflation. The price of the ticket has increased disproportionately to real income. Steaks today should be made available with a payment plan. Four people eating out with drinks and a tip can easily reach $120.00, even in the most moderate economic areas of our great nation.

Eat out even once per week, and we're talking some real money. The problem is, we aren't talking about once per week. I have many friends that eat out a minimum of one meal per DAY. We can kill two birds with one stone here: save money, and lose weight by eating our own cooking. "That's it, I've heard everything from this lunatic that I can stand. I was buying into the house and car ideas, and even considering asking the kids to help pay for their college, but I am NOT eating at home, and that's that!" I didn't say you *had* to. "Well you were insinuating it." Geez, give me a chance.

What my wife and I started doing was inviting ourselves out to eat at our friends' and kids' homes. We eat and go home and they clean up the mess. Okay, it's not exactly like that. What we really have done is talk to our friends and our kids about the cost of eating out. For the price of one prime rib dinner at the restaurant, we can serve four prime rib dinners at home. Ours is better. We aren't rushed, we don't feel like we need to hurry in order to vacate the table, and we have a nice visit and a pleasant evening together.

If you want a cocktail or wine before dinner, it is cheaper to buy a liquor store than to order drinks in most restaurants. We take turns hosting the occasion so that you don't have to eat at home (I told you). This can be particularly enjoyable if you get into barbeque. Women love barbeques, because men are expected to cook. That's why women buy men barbeques the size of small trucks for gifts, and the men are so gullible that they think it's macho to cook on them, because the girls can't handle the big rigs. You gotta love it. Barbeque is required by law to be served on paper plates, and therefore creates very little mess — and what can I say, I'll take mine medium rare.

I don't want you to stop eating at the restaurants all together. That wouldn't be any fun. But try the friends and family plan without having to use your Visa card to pay for it.

I said in the beginning of this chapter that I had about beat the vehicle and home drum as much as you could stand. I changed my mind. The housing thing is soooo important that I want to wrap up this chapter with another blurb about it, just so you really will take a hard look at where you personally stand in that largest category of debt.

If you have a *home* that you enjoy and one that you want to remain in long term, and if you have a manageable mortgage that has fewer years remaining than your expected lifetime, you're probably alright. However, if you are scraping by with a long-term mortgage, counting on the value of your home going up and at the same time your wages increasing, "alright" is not a word that comes to mind.

Be careful how much of your net income is attributed to your overall home costs. If you have an adjustable rate mortgage, interest only, or a piggy back loan that depends on your home increasing in value and, at the same time, your wages going up to make the payment — consider selling. Don't bet on rising home prices and wages. If you think that is going to happen, go back and read the beginning chapters. Consider how far off I could possibly be and then sell that overpriced shelter.

For all practical purposes, the housing market has topped out for this trip. The roller coaster is nearing the top of the grade, and after that, she's all downhill. Some of the brightest financial minds in America concur with that opinion. Even if the housing market simply levels out, those counting on inflated home prices for salvation will be in serious trouble.

Going back to Chapter 1, you will remember that I once lived in an area where there were 1,200 vacant homes after the bust came in the early '80s. Don't look now, but it's coming again. Every corner of this nation will be different. There may be some areas that are nearly unscathed, while total devastation could occur in others. Don't bet your retirement on which area you are living in. When it becomes common knowledge that housing has peaked, selling at that point will be nearly impossible without sustaining losses. In some areas, it won't be possible to sell at all.

Brutal advice, huh? Not nearly as brutal as losing your home in foreclosure or watching your dreams of becoming a Permanent Vacationer disappear with the decline of this ridiculous housing market. Consider the size of your home, and your ability to manage it as taxes and utilities continue to increase. Large homes, with large taxes and large utility bills, will not be the desire of future generations.

I'm going to move on and try to give the young folks some information that they can use to make the best of the debts that we will be gifting them as we depart the working scene. Maybe we could just say, "I don't know what those kids did to mess this all up, it was alright when we left." Then...maybe not.

CHAPTER 16

FOR THE KIDS: A SURVIVAL GUIDE

IN THIS CHAPTER, I am speaking directly to all of you young people who will be left with the mess that your parents and grandparents created. That includes Yours Truly. As a rank and file baby boomer, I, like the other 78 million boomers that range from age 43 to 61, have pretty well muddled things up for you. Did we do it on purpose? I'll try and crawfish out of that category; we did it *with* purpose. I don't believe that most of us approached the subject with malicious intent — at least not in the beginning. Having had certain knowledge of the consequences of our actions, would make us culpable. And we don't want to be culpable. All we wanted were big houses, big cars, big vacations, and a long retirement, while at the same time, being able to say that we were thinking of you. Ha-ha.

At the very least, we don't want to recognize our actions as being outright hostile to our own children and grandchildren. Therefore we have arrived at this juncture under the all-encompassing mantra of "leaving it a better place for you to live." In reality, we were trying to keep up with the neighbors and buy everything that we could get our hands on. But leaving the world a better place for our kids sounds more responsible. We left you a car with an empty tank.

I would assume that several of the older folks are already thinking, "If I had read this chapter first, I would have banned it from my kids. The nerve of this dimwit, suggesting that I purposely created a bad situation for my children. It's preposterous! We bought the 4,000-square-foot house and the diesel-pusher motor home to make our kids lives better." I guess we're just not that good at admitting our mistakes.

I recently read that today's kids will be the first generation in America who will not be able to live at a higher standard than their parents. I'm afraid to even ask how this is being measured. I'm sure it has something to do with buying stuff. In other words, you can't buy more "stuff" than your parents did. That may be the single best thing that has ever happened to you. The real possibility exists that your inability to purchase more instant gratification may actually leave you time to have a life. I helped to create this quandary, and what I offer you, as some repentance, is insight into making lemonade out of the world's largest lemon.

Debt, of course, is the single most terrible animal in this jungle that you are entering. Debt is the King Kong of the ruling factors. It will drag you down like quicksand and reduce your life to one that requires relentless work and stress to keep your fiscal head above water. Yet debt has been prescribed as the cure-all for what ails you.

The distancing between the "haves and have nots," in my opinion, is on a record-setting pace. Middle America is shrinking with every day that goes by. At some point, every one of you will come to that proverbial fork in the road, and the decision of which road you take will determine which side of the division between the have and have nots that you will be on. The fork that I'm talking about has one road that appears to be a well-traveled, four-lane highway, and leads to incurring useless debt for instant gratification. The other road is not nearly as well traveled, and leads to planning for the good life. A life that is still very much within reach in America, for those who chose *not* to follow the road of convention.

I have talked about convention and being normal throughout this book. "Normal" is described by *Webster's* as "conforming with an accepted standard." Such as, "The majority of my friends are hopelessly in debt, so I'll conform to the same standard in an effort to be normal." And you'll meet the same fate. But, look at the bright side — you'll have a lot of company in the ensuing misery.

On the island of Vanuatu, there is a tribe whose men tie various lengths of vines around their ankles and jump off high wooden

towers headfirst in a ceremonial event to see who can come clos-
est to the ground without actually being killed. Another tribe,
in Africa, proves their manhood by hunting a lion with nothing
more than a spear and shield. Uh-huh. I personally don't care to
partake in those festivities. But, for the participants, it's normal.
The next time you want to practice being normal, think about
taking on that lion; debt just eats you slower.

Debt is what keeps this false economic charade going, temporarily. Ever-mounting national and personal debt is what it
takes to try and get one more mile out of a system that was
never designed to work long term. Had it not been for debt being the mainstay for holding up the economy, there would have
been a campaign of "just say NO" to debt long before the slogan was applied to cigarettes and drugs. Debt has ruined lives
tenfold in comparison to drugs and cigarettes, but for a much
better cause — growth.

Whether its debt, drugs, cigarettes, or jumping out of a tree
with a vine tied to your leg, being normal in keeping up with
your peers can have some serious drawbacks. Finding a new
group to hang with seems a whole lot more sensible. If you practice convention (doing what everyone else is doing), you can expect to have the same measure of success as the group who chose
the beaten path when they came to that fork in the road.

There is a necessity for some debt in America. The most important factor is the *level* and *type* of debt that you choose to incur. I want to assure you that I have no intention of suggesting
a life of poverty and hopelessness — nothing like that.

In order to build anything, including a life, you have to start
out with a solid foundation: in this instance, a realistic plan that
you believe in. You need to figure out where it is that you are
going or what it is that you are building before you can start,
otherwise you might build the roof first with no walls to put it
on. I know, you've heard it all before, but none-the-less, I think
that we can agree that if you don't know where you are going,
you simply aren't going to get there.

What do you really want out of life? What are your interests? What makes you happy? What is your passion? I'm

betting that it isn't working the remainder of your adult life at a job that you don't enjoy, for the principal purpose of making interest payments. Behaving as an average American consumer by purchasing everything within your grasp and maxing out your credit limit may be what holds up this ludicrous economy, but remember, if you participate, it's you who will be standing under that debt load when the roof caves in.

Okay, here you are with most of your adult life ahead of you and the prospects, as you see them, are somewhat dim, and I'm not making you feel any better. But, what you see may be clouded by misperception. Falsely channeled perception creates mirages; visions that don't really exist. Most of our beliefs are directed by perception, primarily that of *perceived* happiness.

That being said, if you have a perception of life that is a mirage, and you follow that vision, you are pursuing a life that doesn't really exist. *For the perceiver is the believer, and to the believer, it is truth* — Mike Folkerth

If your perception is false, that is where the trouble begins. Following a false belief may well rob you of your life. This might seem like lots of mumbo jumbo, but hang with me, and I'll make some sense of it all.

Let's take the example of believing that a new car will be the path to eternal happiness. The advertisements reveal that and more. A new car will make you a date magnet. It will relieve all of the stress that work creates. A new car will make you one happy camper — for about 30 days. After which you are one cold, rained-out camper that wishes you had stayed home. So it's an illusion then, and it steered you off in the wrong direction. A very costly direction.

Ask anyone who has bought a new car if it makes them happy to shell out half of their income on a vehicle that is going down in value like a dropped rock. I'd say the answer is NO, unless you ask someone who is still in the 30-day Cinderella period that follows the initial purchase. The initial 30-day period of new auto ownership occurs just prior to the point of being whacked over the head by reality. What did you trade 60 to 84 extra large monthly payments on a depreciating asset for?

A big chunk of your life, but what the hey — you have lots of life left, right?

Don't trade life for stuff. It's a real bad trade. It's all a matter of perception. Instead of having the impression that your buddy is one cool dude or chick with that brand new car, change that to your buddy is one dumb dude or chick who apparently missed general math all together. Have fun, not debt. Buy that two- or three-year-old car that we talked about in an earlier chapter. This is survival for your generation. Be a survivor and have a good life.

All it takes is self-confidence, and I know that together, we're going to achieve that requirement. Knowledge and self-confidence are a package deal. Once you know what you want out of life, and once you figure out that debt and the false promise of instant happiness isn't going to get you there, life will take on a whole new meaning.

Many years ago, a friend observed that I took a lot of ridicule for riding my bike rather than driving a new car in my then-home of Talkeetna, Alaska. However, he would also make the contradictory, but humorous, observation that I rode my bike over to the airport to get into my private plane. I loved that airplane, and it brought me great pleasure. At the time, a used airplane cost less than a new car, not to mention that airplanes continued to go up in value and cars continued to go down. Flying was my passion and giving up the image that a new car provided was an easy choice for me.

Where did I get the money to buy an airplane? I saved it by owning a cheap used car and a bicycle. I saved and paid cash for that used airplane. Why would anyone ridicule me for that? They didn't have an airplane!

My life has been anything but dull. I was blessed with an early understanding that was taught to me by my parents and others who were influential in my youth that possessions are not important, and they can come and go. Knowledge and self-confidence are the real treasures of life. By understanding that the measure of a person cannot be made by observing what they have been able to purchase, is a key factor to a better life. I have always, and with purpose, lived below my means, yet few have had the experiences that life has given me. Or, I should say, that I have *taken* from life.

Living below your means is a powerful subject that deserves a little more ink. It does take an extra measure of self-confidence and knowledge to practice living below your means. A few years ago, when he was a teenager, one of my boys asked, "You and Mom are doing alright aren't you?" I said, "Sure, but what do you mean?" He said, "I mean financially. Things are going pretty well, aren't they?" I said, "Yes, things are going very well." He then looked puzzled and said, "Then why don't you buy a new house?"

You see, my son saw that most people who had some measure of financial success were buying new houses and, therefore, considered purchasing one a near requirement for publicly announcing ones current financial and social status. Today, he understands why we didn't buy a new house. The one we had was paid for. The money that would have bought us a new house was instead invested into commercial-rental, and investment property. In time, the income from those properties afforded us free time and fierce independence.

The continual theme of this writing is that once you achieve happiness, there is nothing more to be gained. That's it; you're at the top of the mountain. Staying there is the trick. Without happiness, all the money and possessions in the world are worthless. Being happy is there for the taking, but fraught with illusions.

You will soon be living in a world that will be a dramatic change from that of your parents. By all government accounts, Social Security and Medicare will be broke beyond repair prior to your golden years, yet you will continue to pay into it until it falls flat on its face. These facts have been known for years and years, but nothing is done to correct it. Why? I'd say that pure unadulterated selfishness and greed defines the situation nicely.

Those who believe that they can take the ill-gotten gains and get out before the collapse have some unfounded, contrived belief that "they" have it coming, and refuse to correct a known catastrophic problem. Do you remember the thought-provoking question, "If a tree falls in the forest and no one is around to hear it, did it make a sound?" Same theme: "If Social Security and Medicare fail after I'm dead, did they really fail?"

The answer to both questions is, of course, YES! Will it have an adverse effect on those near to retirement, or on their 4,000-square-foot homes, new SUVs, or Country Club membership? No. Therefore, as a whole, the older generations aren't that concerned about how you survive in the aftermath.

Welcome to the me, me, me generation. Believing "The Biggest Lie Ever Believed" is much easier if it doesn't personally have a negative effect on the person doing the believing. Unfortunately, that includes most politicians and Big Business execs, who are in a position to affect meaningful change, but have much to gain by not doing so.

We could blame all of the problems that you will face on the government, but then we are the government and should have done something a long time ago. So, blaming the government is no good. That would make the whole situation somehow our fault. I know! We can blame it on the Tooth Fairy, because we don't have any real control over the Tooth Fairy. So that's it then, the Tooth Fairy robbed so much money out from under your pillows when you were little that it has shortchanged Social Security and Medicare, and now those programs are going broke. And we can't even find the Tooth Fairy to prosecute her! So, you see, it isn't our fault after all. That sounds silly, but in reality, not nearly as silly as our total disregard for dealing with the very real and KNOWN problems that your generation will be facing.

I could go on railing about how we got here and who's to blame, but I covered that in the first 11 chapters. Regardless of the route that we took to arrive, we are here, all the same. The question that remains is: how are you going to make what we leave you work? Social Security and Medicare may be the least of your problems.

The physical impossibility of exponential growth is far more threatening. Funding our social obligations today can't be done without incurring enormous deficits. Funding the social costs of the retiring baby boomers will prove impossible. You can read that any day of the week. What's the solution that we have given you? MORE GROWTH. You people better get cracking. Just work a little harder and a little longer, and it will be just fine — for *us* that is. You, personally, have a mess.

"Continuing to do the same thing year after year and expecting to eventually achieve different results" is one definition of insanity. So if you're not nuts, don't do what past generations have been doing. Repeating the same behavior will only worsen the situation, and you have enough problems without creating more. On the other hand, don't ask us what to do; we apparently don't know. At least we don't want to know, because we strongly suspect that it could create some additional stress in our lives. And we would rather create some additional stress in your lives, if you don't mind.

I hope that you have read this entire book: it is important to understand how and why we are at this juncture, in order not to repeat the same dumb errors that those who preceded you did (not to name any names). Coming to grips with it seems far too challenging for my generation, primarily because we want sooo bad to believe "The Biggest Lie Ever Believed," and get out unscathed with all the loot. Don't confuse us with the facts. The ill-conceived belief that growth would answer the bell for the next one thousand years has not worked out real well for you.

Much of what you have been taught, and consequently believe, was necessary to fuel the fire of consumerism, even though it was devastating to your future. The new cars, computers, homes, electronics, games, and gimmicks were all necessary to stimulate the impossible required growth. So now what? Let's ride in my magic time machine to a place where you can live the best life possible under the circumstances. We're not going forward, we're going back. We left reality back there somewhere, and we need to find it.

Let's start by saying work is overrated; maybe not for your employer, but darn sure for you. Americans spend more time at work than any other people in the world. By utilizing all the wonderful electronics of today's business world, you can talk on the phone and work 24-7. By purchasing everything that your maximum credit will allow, you can accumulate more possessions than you physically have time to manage.

Since it has become necessary for couples to work full-time in order to support the average American family's debt, we have reached the enviable maximum possible production and debt load of a human being. That's wonderful for you, huh? I didn't think so. When we look at it like that, it seems somewhat ridiculous, doesn't it? All the same, that's where we are. That's what it took to maintain the growth necessary to keep your current elected officials in office, and America treading water. We'll soon hit the peak of this ill conceived strategy.

What is on the other side of the peak? That's right — a valley, all downhill. If you can't produce more and more in a society that counts on producing more and more, what happens? Before you answer that, I have a better question: why would you want to? Really, why do you want to go on participating in this madness? Whoever made up the rules anyway? Is it really necessary to work faster and produce more every year, until it just isn't possible to work faster and produce more every year? I'll give you a little hint. Has anyone ever told you, "You better enjoy your childhood; it's the best part of your life?" The same person that told you that helped make up the rules, at least they have been following them.

How about we analyze that statement regarding childhood being the best part of your life? That would mean that through experience, those who told you that have determined that adulthood isn't all that much fun. What a shame. That would also tell you that whoever told you that was assuming that you weren't going to be having all that much fun in adulthood either. At least they weren't willing to correct their own situation, and they had taken for granted that you weren't willing to correct yours either.

That would also tell you that the person who told you that adulthood wasn't going to be all that much fun was following the crowd, regardless of the consequences. If you are even a little bit concerned that adult life is going to be a letdown after childhood, I'd strongly consider a new plan. What does it take to be different? Yeah, you got it: knowledge, self-confidence, and the less-traveled path. Question EVERYTHING, and wait for an acceptable answer. "Because that's what everyone else does" is *not* an acceptable answer.

If I could do just one thing to try and help you, it would be to give you the knowledge and self-confidence to change your life. If being normal isn't all that much fun, then by all means, don't be. Question yourself — What do you want out of life? If your answer is working and struggling endlessly to hold onto all your earthly possessions, be my guest and have at it. But if the answer to your question is to live an adventurous, happy, and fulfilling life, don't copy the people who already admitted to you that it will get worse as time goes along. Give yourself a break, change your focus. The greatest single thing that we are leaving you is freedom of choice.

It's difficult to go against convention. That great persuader — peer pressure — is one tough customer. The following saying is one that I use often and hope that you will adopt. I used it earlier in the book, but no truer words were ever spoken than those of Davy Crockett, who simply said, "Always be sure you are right, then go ahead." Don't let the actions and opinions of your peers steer you wrong when you *know* that you are right.

Davy Crockett also said, We "...must not permit our respect for the dead or our sympathy for a part of the living to lead us into an act of injustice to the balance of the living." Davy Crockett died March 6, 1836, defending the Alamo. But what he said could easily be applied to what past generations have done to you. Hopefully your generation will spawn another Davy Crockett to stand up for your rights. Principled men of Mr. Crockett's stature are in short supply today. The youth of this nation badly need a champion at the highest level of our Federal Government.

No one can change the past, but you can change your future. Be it cars, homes, computers, electronics, boats, snowmobiles, or a myriad of other high-cost offerings, don't get suckered in. The associated debt will take over your life.

Don't rush to buy a home with the idea that if you don't plunge into lifelong debt now, you may never be able to afford your own home. If that is the future, then so be it. It isn't the end of the world, trust me. I'd trade free time and independence over the Taj Mahal. If you can afford a home while remaining within the guidelines that I laid out in the earlier chapters, go for it. Home ownership can have the advantage of fixing your housing costs at a known sum. However, be very cautious of buying at the top of the roller coaster. At the date of this writing, there are furious home buyers who paid as much as $100,000 more for the same home that is being sold today as existing record inventorys are heavily discounted, due mainly to falling sales.

Think about eductional costs. At 17 or 18, many people don't really know what they want to do with the rest of their lives. And you don't need to know. Search around, and the answer will find you. The cost of an education in a field that you find doesn't suit you later on can have far-reaching implications, not the least of which is feeling that you need to remain in a profession that you dislike. Consider a vocational education, if that is what you really want. Don't allow peer pressure and what others want for you to influence what you want for yourself. Choose a line of work that you will enjoy and one that makes sense for the lifestyle that you desire.

Over the last 20 years, the belief that college was the only noble route to success has raised plumbers' and electricians' wages to $50.00 per hour, while college psychology grads are unable to find work. Be what you want to be, so long as it is honorable and does not burden others. If you need to take a few years to test the water before you attend college, do it; just don't incur debt to a point that education later in life becomes impossible. Hold on to that financial freedom. Adhering to someone else's rendition of the Amercian Dream just may not fit your clothes, if you know what I mean.

I certainly am not inferring that education is a bad thing. Far from it. I am only stating that a university education is not the only way to a happy life and an honorable career. Try not to work in a field that you don't enjoy. Life will be a real bummer, and that former line about your childhood being the best part of your life will become oh-so-true. We all have to work at something, just don't let your work and your lust for material wealth become more important than your life.

Get together with your friends and relatives that are facing the same challenges that you are. Talk about the things that you would like to change so that you can live a better life. You will be astounded at the interest that you can generate in redefining the good life. Having support for and sharing new-found ideas is something that we all need. It is my opinion that an entirely new culture will develop that embraces the less debt, more fun, and fewer work hours concept. Communities will be established that foster those beliefs. Be a frontrunner, and help to develop those communities.

Consider saving for yourself rather than counting on the Federal Government providing you with Social Security or your employer coming through with retirement. If those things come through, great, but have a plan "B." In my previous two examples of buying a used car rather than new, and, obtaining a 15- rather than a 30-year mortgage on a modest *home*, a person could *self-finance* retirement by investing the realized cash differences in a tax-deferred investment vehicle that returned an average of 7%.

Invest wisely — if it seems too good to be true, it probably is. I personally have little confidence in the stock market. Investing is a tricky business, get help from someone that you trust, and who has a track record of making good, conservative choices. Always have some cash savings to get you through a tough time or to deal with an unexpected expense.

You just can't do these things and, at the same time, buy every gadget that is dangled in front of you. Maintain a debt level that allows leisure time. Avoid high paid entertainment and restaurant meals. Get together with those new friends that share your concept and cook out. Go biking, camping, canoeing, hiking, cross-country skiing, sledding, swimming, or a million other things that have a low cost and high return.

Talk openly and constantly about your goals of maintaining a simple, sustainable, and enjoyable lifestyle with your spouse, friends, family, significant other, or whomever you are close to. There are thousands of people who will share your concepts and views. And those are the people that you need to associate with, not the buy-now-and-pay-later crowd. You can't fly with the eagles and roost with turkeys. The absolute commitment to living a more leisurely and invigorating lifesyle, and the categorical knowledge that you are correct in doing so, is all powerful.

One area that I want to be perfectly clear about is that under no circumstances do I suggest in any way, shape, or form that it is mandatory for you to live a passive, mundane lifestyle. Quite the contrary: Get out there and *take* what life and this great country have to offer. I think you will find that following my past suggestions will leave you with a lot more time and money to do just that.

And finally, when the time comes, raise your children to be happy, not to be the subjects of "The Biggest Lie Ever Believed."

ABOUT THE AUTHOR

Mike Folkerth does not base his writing from borrowed text book examples, but rather from insight gained from his real life experiences. These include, real estate broker, developer, private real estate fund manager, auctioneer, Alaskan bush pilot, restaurateur, U.S. Navy veteran, professional writer and general entrepreneur.

Raised in the heartland of Indiana's farming and industry, Mike identifies closely with the plight of middle class America, and the coming life-altering troubles that the "finest group of people on earth" will soon be facing. Mike lives with his wife Cathy in Cedaredge, Colorado.